# Being With Jesus

## Devotions for the Growing Disciple



WINNIPEG. MB Kindred Productions HILLSBORO, KS

Kindred Productions is the publishing arm for the Mennonite Brethren Churches. Kindred publishes, promotes and markets print and mixed media resources that help shape our Christian faith and discipleship from the Mennonite Brethren perspective.

**Being with Jesus**



Published simultaneously by Kindred Productions,
Winnipeg MB R2L 2E5 and
Kindred Productions, Hillsboro KS 67063

Cover and book design by Makus Design, Winnipeg MB
Photo on page 9 by Carlos De Le Rosa

Printed in Canada by The Christian Press

---

**National Library of Canada Cataloguing in Publication**

Baergen, Carol, 1963-
Being with Jesus : devotions for the growing disciple / Carol Baergen.

Includes bibliographical references.
ISBN 0-921788-98-3

1. Devotional exercises. I. Title.

BV4832.3.B33 2004 242 C2004-902418-3

**Dedicated to**

my husband Evan who encourages my dreams and walk with God. To my children Jon, Katie and Ellie who refine my walk with God. To my parents who taught me about myself and loved me through many trials. To my church family at Cedar Park Church in Delta, BC, who give me room, time and encouragement to grow.

# Contents

# ACKNOWLEDGEMENTS

First and foremost, thank you God, for in the midst of pain you brought forth this work from the ashes of lost dreams.

Thank you to Sharon Johnson, Director of Adult Ministries, Canadian Conference of MB Churches. I am inspired by your knowledge, wisdom, deep love for the Lord and your gentle, valiant spirit.

Thank you to my husband, Evan Baergen and my mom, Janet Ebert, who read endless drafts and offered many suggestions, to Shelli Bothamley for reviewing the first draft, to Irene Emery for dictionary and thesaurus help (and emotional support!), to Dave Swan and Ed Wiens of the Adult Ministry team at Cedar Park for your contributions and dedication in working with me, and to Pastor Dave Esau of Cedar Park Church for contributing to the book and for giving me opportunities for growth and leadership.

# INTRODUCTION

Following Jesus is like white water rafting. He is the capable, committed guide, essential for our survival. Other rafters are critically important. Everyone must learn to navigate and to remain safely in the raft. There are moments of terror, exhilaration, tranquility, discouragement and achievement—all of which describe the incredible adventure of entrusting oneself to our Guide for the journey.

Jesus approached his first disciples with the invitation, "Come with me...I will make you...I will show you how" (Mark 1:17). Jesus continues to extend this invitation to join him in this life-changing, revolutionary adventure called discipleship.

Discipleship involves much more than simply gaining knowledge. It is the process of transformation of the heart. It is choosing to **be with Jesus** in order to learn to be like him, in the power he gives. It is responding to God's work in our lives, with his initiative making our transformation possible.

The *Description of a Growing Disciple* (DGD) is an attempt to describe who we are becoming as devoted followers of Jesus, as evidenced by our changing behavior. While the DGD is not exhaustive, it focuses on six pairs of character qualities which complete the sentence: "A growing disciple is someone who is ...."

A growing disciple is someone who is...

Captivated and Committed
Thriving and Thirsting
Bonded and Building
Inviting and Influencing
Discerning and Disarming
Purposeful and Persevering [1]

Over the next six weeks, we will explore the six paired attributes with the aim of helping us become more devoted disciples of Christ. Each chapter consists of five daily devotions, with stories for your weekend reflection.

Each day's reading begins with biblical references. I encourage you to read the full passage listed, remembering that it is God's message to you. A short narrative follows, to provoke understanding, contemplation and the desire to grow. Several questions accompany the narrative to help you reflect on what you have read. If God brings other questions to mind, prayerfully consider his questions first—he is the Guide on our journey. A prayer is written at the end to guide you back to God's presence—the best place for a growing disciple to be!

My prayer is that this devotional will draw you to seek God more deeply, passionately and fully. May the devotions remind you of what it means to be a disciple of Christ. I pray that with the joy set before you, you will focus on the goal, losing sight of all that would hinder you. May the facts that God himself pursues you, that Jesus himself died for you and that the Holy Spirit works alongside you, help you find passion and strength to become a *growing* disciple of Christ!

Carol Baergen

1. Excerpted from the Description of a Growing Disciple. Copyright 2004 Adult Ministries, Canadian Conference of MB Churches.

* Some of the narratives are based on true stories and some are fictional.

# CAPTIVATED AND COMMITTED

**Scriptures:**

Matthew 22:36-40; John 21:15-17; Revelation 2:1-7; Luke 7:36-48

**God's Initiative:**

*We love, because he first loved us.* 1 John 4:19

**Description:**

A person who believes in Jesus increasingly loves him with "heart, soul, mind and strength," and is committed to growing as a disciple, regardless of the cost.

**Evidence:**

- Understands the scriptural basis for, and is confident of, a personal saving relationship with Christ.
- Feels a growing love for God, which motivates increasing obedience.
- Expresses faith and is keen to talk about life in Christ.

## Be IN GOD'S WORD

*Knowing that you were not redeemed with corruptible things, like silver or gold...but with the precious blood of Christ, as of a lamb, without blemish and without spot.* 1 Peter 1:18 – 19 NKJV

## Be IN OUR STORY

"Jesus' purpose was to die in our place." The preacher says the words so softly. I have heard them thundered from the pulpit so many times before! Today the softness of his voice and the tone of awe pierces my heart. Lord, when I was first saved I was so thankful. Then over the years as I moved into ministry I began to think you were so lucky to have me in your service. I was so creative, so willing, such a "good catch." Now, sitting here today, I am ashamed at my selfishness. I cannot lift my head and look at the cross. The tears run down my cheeks as I realize again how much you love me! I can hardly speak of your name at work. Yet you so willingly left heaven and the close fellowship of God and angels to be human with all that entails—the physical needs, the mental stresses, and the spiritual journey of being human. You did all that for me? You were mocked, ridiculed, beaten and hung on a cross, naked...all for me?

Today I am suddenly struck, Lord, as I realize the separation from God you went through. I can only know a tiny taste of the pain in my days of wilderness. To know God fully and for all eternity and then to be separated.... Your pain is unbearable in my mind; my heart aches, my hands shake and I sob! How could I be so careless, so thoughtless about your sacrifice for me? My head knows that you did this for the world; that you would have done it even if there was only me to save. Not the church-attender, the Bible study leader, but "me" with sinful thoughts and ways, with the lazy way I approach you, with the careless words that spew from this mouth that proclaims to love you. It is truly a wonder. Amidst my sobs today only a soft whisper comes from my quivering lips and in unspeakable awe I whisper, "I'm sorry. I forgot. Thank you!"

## *Be* IN THE QUESTIONS

1. Who would you die for like this?
2. If you were innocent, would you die for the guilty? If you were a rich king, would you die for the poor, lowly peasant?
3. If you were Creator of the heavens and the earth and every power was at your command, would you keep your mouth closed and die for those who turn their back on you?

## *Be* IN GOD'S PRESENCE

Lord, I come to you in prayer and ask that your Holy Spirit would speak to me. I am coming to the cross—a place that if I have asked you to be my Saviour, I have come to at least once before. A place that as a follower of Christ I come to every day to ask for forgiveness of my sins. A place that has become more ritual than a sharp reminder of the reality; more of a quick pit stop than a place to stop, stay and be silent. I did not want it this way—but life is busy and matters are pressing. Help me to Stop, Look and Listen today as I walk to the cross! Amen

*Stay a while...listen.*

# Day 2

## *Be* IN GOD'S WORD

*We love because he first loved us.* I John 4:19

## *Be* IN OUR STORY

My husband turns to me. "You've been so quiet on this trip. The wheels in your mind must be turning—tell me what's up."

I smile. "How would you express your relationship with God?"

"You got me!" he laughs. "Of all the things I thought we were going to talk about, this wasn't one of them."

"Well, let's talk about it."

My husband thinks for a moment. "It's about desire, something that gives you a thrill, that challenges you to pursue it. My desire for God is growing and becoming more of a priority in my life. When something is a priority, it gets more dedication, more time and effort from me. And consciousness."

"Consciousness?"

"It's like my triathlons. Not a day goes by that I don't think about triathlons. I make many choices in life in order to do well in them. My food choices, exercises, even my activities get put into the perspective of training. I put effort into it every day. I read about triathlons, think about them, dream and talk about them—and it's the same with God. And, just like my triathlons, the more I do, the more I want to do. The more I see what God has done for me—leaving heaven to be human in a fallen world, dying deliberately in my place so I could be restored to relationship with God—the more I want to know him."

"Okay. You've talked about knowledge, but what about your emotions?"

He smiles. "Yes, there are emotions involved." (I knew it!) "They just aren't all over the place like yours."

"Hey! I resemble—I mean resent—that!" We laugh at the old joke before I speak again. "For me, a relationship with God starts with what I know about Jesus, but it is so much more. When my knowledge becomes experience, I am captivated by him. I experience wonder and awe at his grace and unconditional love, and at the mystery of believing. I think of Jesus not only as my solid faithful redeemer, but also as fun and adventuresome. Remember when we first fell in love? We couldn't stop thinking about each other. We lived for the moments when we could be together. That's how I feel about Jesus—and it's growing!"

"Well," he says. "I see what you're saying, and I would describe my relationship with Christ as captivation too. My emotions play an essential role, but they aren't the driving force—they're more like feedback."

"So, we can both be captivated by God—only with me it is more emotionally driven and with you it's more intellectual?"

"Yes, but don't forget that both sorts of faith are important. I'm often drawn to your openness with God. Your excitement and zeal are contagious. And you have relied on me, especially when you are having a difficult time, to remind you of the truths of the Bible. So, we both grow in those areas. Look at the mountains," he continues, sweeping his hand toward the view. "My expression of faith is like that—solid. Look at the river there—your expression of faith is more like the river, giving life wherever it goes."

## *Be* IN THE QUESTIONS

1. What is the basis for your relationship with God? How have you experienced his love for you?
2. Is your love for God more emotionally or intellectually driven? In what ways do you seek balance to your "faith style"?
3. How can you ensure that God remains your first love? How can you express this love?

## *Be* IN GOD'S PRESENCE

Lord, in human relationships, love grows and changes from exciting newness and passion into a solid relationship, through turbulent times that require deep commitment and joys which are shared. Help me to see my relationship with you in the same way. God, you loved us first and completely in the life and death of your son Jesus Christ. Thank you for loving me and desiring a relationship with me. In whatever faith style I have, may you be my first love. Amen.

## *Be* IN GOD'S WORD

*"Love the Lord your God with all your heart and with all your soul and with all your mind. This is the first and greatest commandment."* Matthew 22:37-38

## *Be* IN OUR STORY

For months I have been struggling to understand what it means to love God with all your heart, soul, mind and strength. Then, the phone rings. It is my adored Dad.

"The news is bad," he says. "The tumor they thought was benign is actually cancerous."
"What?!" I whisper.
"I have cancer." As he talks, I revert from a 40 year old to a four year old in two seconds. The tears come and my spirit flees to the throne of God, begging him: "Not my Dad! Not my children's Grandpa!" I pull myself together enough to talk things through with my dad and then ask if I can pray for him. As soon as I start to pray, words choke in my throat—there is something about being before God that makes me lose myself in open abandon as the tears come flooding. My Dad assures me he will fight the cancer and we say our goodbyes.

I hang up and run to God in prayer, babbling so fast I am incoherent. I think about the verse that says that the Spirit interprets the groaning of our spirit—good thing, I am thinking, even God may have trouble with the thousand thoughts and emotions flooding my being. Then I realize: this is it! This is what loving God is like! We simply involve him so much in our day that we automatically run to him with our hurts, joys and fears. I can run to God's lap with tears, and he will comfort me as a parent does a hurting child. I don't hesitate or stop to consider whether what I am feeling is valid or proper—I am in pain and I need my heavenly Father now! Loving God with all our heart, soul, mind and strength is not some theological mystery—it is making him a part of every aspect of our lives, by turning our thoughts and attention to him, waiting for him to respond in love. There's no secret formula—it's love. It isn't just on Sundays or special days—in all days and all ways, we love God with all we've got!

## *Be* IN THE QUESTIONS

1. How can we love God by remembering to include him in all aspects of life?
2. Why do we hesitate to voice "darker" emotions to God, and why do we think about whether (wonder if) our feelings are proper?
3. When have you experienced God's love for you (and yours for him) most clearly? How can this experience teach you to love God each day?

## *Be* IN GOD'S PRESENCE

Lord, sometimes I forget what loving you is all about. Worse, I forget your love for me. And even still, you love and forgive me—the me with sinful thoughts, careless words and lazy ways. You want me to invite you into my joys and heartaches, to bear my burdens and to know my heart. Lord, don't let me forget you. Help me to love you with all my heart, soul, mind and strength. Amen.

## *Be* IN GOD'S WORD

*When they had finished eating, Jesus said to Simon Peter, "Simon, son of John, do you truly love me more than these?" "Yes Lord," he said, "you know that I love you." Jesus said, "Feed my lambs."* John 21:15-17

## *Be* IN OUR STORY

"Petering out" is an expression I relate to! Often, I start off with great energy and excitement, and then...peter out. I wonder if this expression comes from the apostle Peter's early behavior—when things were going well, he had all the words and enthusiasm, but no "stick-to-itiveness" when the going got rough. I can sympathize with Peter. I find it easy to say I love Jesus, but hard to live out. Is it enough to have accepted Jesus as Savior? Is it enough to have accepted him as Lord? To go to church and help out where I can?

The reality is that Jesus wants more than my most righteous actions. Not that he demands it or holds back his love if I don't willingly love him, but he does want more of me.

*For I desire mercy, not sacrifice, and acknowledgment of God rather than burnt offerings* (Hosea 6:6). This verse reminds me that God wants me to do more than "sacrifice," offering the modern equivalents of good deeds. He wants my devotion and loyalty. He wants my obedience to flow from my genuine recognition of God, instead of duty. Cain and Abel are an example of this: both brought sacrifices but Abel's was accepted because he brought it with the right intent, while Cain's was not because he brought his as an outward display, without love for God. In the New Testament, Jesus praised deeds, not because they were great in the world's view, but because they were done with the right heart: the widow's offering (Mark 12:41-44), the anointing of Jesus (Matthew 26:6-13) and the parable of the two sons (Matthew 21:28-32).

The fact is that Jesus wants me to be like him, willing to give up everything to live entirely for God. In a society of plenty, where comfort is often the goal, I struggle with the idea of self-sacrifice. Still, Jesus said he would give me life more abundantly. Life isn't always easy, but God never said it was about ease.

While our society also says that faith should be kept in a quiet compartment where it doesn't affect anything else, God tells me, *Love the Lord your God with all your heart and with all your soul and with all your strength* (Deuteronomy 6:5). When you really think about it, is there anything we do in a day that does not involve our heart, mind soul and/or strength? We show our love and devotion for God in everything we do and say and everywhere we go.

## *Be* IN THE QUESTIONS

1. Most people focus on Jesus' questions about Peter's love. Instead, let's recognize that Jesus accepted Peter's word and then gave him work to do. What does this teach us about calling and service for God?
2. If you were to take the Lord out of your secret "church" compartment and love him openly in all parts of your life, what do you think would change?
3. What is the right place for duty and rote obedience in the Christian life?

## *Be* IN GOD'S PRESENCE

Lord, I do love you. Sometimes I am unsure how to express that love. Going to church, serving, participating in this and that—it all feels like a list of chores, instead of a heartfelt gift. Help my mouth to be more willing to say your name anywhere. Help my hands to reach out in service and to remember they are doing a service to you. Please remind my feet that the path they follow may not always be easy, but neither was yours. Encourage me to stay on the path and keep going. Help me to be as enthusiastic about you as I am about my hobbies and friends. Help me not just to say it, but to live it out in my actions, as Peter did. Amen.

# Day 5

## Be IN GOD'S WORD

Psalm 63:1-6

*O God, you are my God, earnestly I seek you; my soul thirsts for you, my body longs for you…I have seen you in the sanctuary and beheld your power and your glory. Because your love is better than life, my lips will glorify you. I will praise you as long as I live.*

Psalm 63:1-4

## Be IN OUR STORY

Sports, television shows, kids, sales—we all talk so easily about these things. We meet on the street, over a meal or even in the foyer of the church and freely discuss these matters. Sometimes, though, I want to talk about spiritual things. I wonder if I am on track with God and what others are experiencing in their relationships with God. What if instead of asking each other, "How are you?" at church, we began inquiring "What's new in your relationship with God?" We could create opportunities to share what God is doing in our lives. We could be held accountable to put effort into knowing God, so we could have a response other than "uhh…nothing much."

If we began to express our experiences with God to each other at church, so we felt relaxed about it, then sharing at work might not seem so hard or out of place. Church is a place to "practice" our faith, to prepare us to be in the world, so I wonder why I feel as nervous to talk about what God is doing in my life at church as I am at the office. Sometimes I act as if God is merely an incidental weekend activity, rather than the center of my life. God does many intimate and incredible wonders in our lives. Maybe it's time to start telling the world so they can know he is alive and well. Maybe we could even start by sharing with each other in the house of God.

So, what's new in *your* relationship with God?

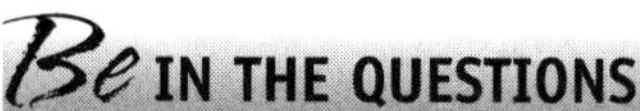

## Be IN THE QUESTIONS

1. Why does conversation about anything else come more easily than talk about God?
2. Why do we hesitate to talk about what God is doing in our lives?
3. If you have not experienced God in any great way this week, seek out someone who did and reassure yourself that God is alive and well.

## Be IN GOD'S PRESENCE

Lord, I love you so much but sometimes I'm still nervous to talk about you. At work I worry they will think I am a fanatic, and at church I'm afraid I won't be spiritual enough. I want to tell people about the ways you surprise me in the day with little things that lighten my heart and remind me of you. I love how you sometimes give me a word through a friend, a verse or a sign on the street. I so easily share frustrations about unanswered prayers with friends from church—help me to be more willing to share what you do for me. Help me to look for you throughout the day, to recognize your hand at work in my life. Amen.

# Weekend stories

## A FAN'S FAITH

I believe hockey is great! I didn't always feel this way though. When I first met my husband, I didn't understand his attraction to hockey—men chasing a little puck back and forth in a cold arena? Then I learned the rules, got to know some of the teams and started to go to the occasional game with my husband. (OK, it was more to be with him than for the game, but still, my interest in hockey grew.)

Lately, I've been eager to go to all the games I can. You see, my husband now works for a company with a suite in GM Place. How I see the game has changed. From where I used to sit in tiny seats with people spilling drinks on you, and a two-mile line for the bathroom, to spacious seats, a couch for visiting, food and a private bathroom—has the game ever improved! Meeting new people, the food and fun are part of the attraction, and the game itself isn't bad after all.

My husband, however, is an avid follower of hockey. He knows all the teams, the players, who's been traded when and where. He has the rules memorized in detail, and only goes to his rulebook on the kitchen counter when he has to explain a technicality to our son. He watches the game with a zealous enthusiasm that even the neighbors can testify to. His schedule is based around hockey—when hockey is on, everything else has to wait. He will pay to drive, park and buy tickets to the game—cost is little object if he gets to be there for the action. Everyone who spends more than five minutes talking to my husband knows that he is a fan—the man can turn any conversation to the topic of hockey. He sticks with his team during the rough times. He will defend the players and the plays. If they gave out fan awards, I would put his name on the list.

If they gave out fan awards for Christianity, I wonder whether I would be on the list? I'm a firm believer in hockey, but I'm not a follower. I don't want to be simply a believer of Jesus, but a die-hard, 100% committed follower—because his is the winning team.

## A CLUE TO A TREASURE HUNT

She said the simplest thing and it shook my world. It was one of those statements that rings in your head for days. You lay awake at night and think about it. You are in the shower and the thought drifts back to you. It's like a clue to a treasure hunt—and you can't let it go.

"Jesus never told the church their commitment was missing; he told them they had left their first love." That was all she said, but something deep inside my soul heard it. The more I thought about it, the more I realized that Jesus had more to say to the religious systems of his day than to the world. It wasn't just the rest of the world who put Jesus to death—it was the religious system. Pilate couldn't understand what Jesus had done wrong so he gave Jesus over to the religious authorities to do with as they wished. They killed him.

But I found myself not casting judgment on the people of Jesus' day, or even on our modern church, but instead questioning my own heart. I could feel that there was great truth, a treasure, or even a mystery in Jesus' message. Had I been all wrong? Had I been approaching my faith like the Pharisees, missing the whole point? I sat quietly listening for God, reading his Word. God began to show me that I had been obedient, but more out of duty. It was time to return to my "first love." I sat and recalled the experience of falling in love with Jesus.

Jesus did not want his followers to be conformed to the religious system of the day because it was about works, arrogance and the letter of the law. Is the church different today? Am I? Instead, he offered treasures of freedom and grace.

I prayed: "Lord, keep that phrase 'return to your first love' ringing in my ears. It has made me look at how I need to serve you differently. It has given me new vision with which to examine my actions. I want to capture the emotion and the drive I had when I first realized your unconditional love for me. Being captivated by who you are is what keeps me committed to you. Amen."

•••••••••••••••••••••••••••••••••

# THRIVING AND THIRSTING

**Scriptures:**

2 Peter 1:3-11; Deuteronomy 5:33; John 15:1-8

**God's Initiative:**

*His divine power has given us everything we need for life and godliness.* 2 Peter 1:3

**Description:**

A person who determines to abide in Christ and is committed to cultivating a growing relationship with God, even in adverse circumstances, so that faith is progressively more vibrant.

**Evidence:**

- Learns to study Scripture, inductively and devotionally.
- Becomes devoted to knowing God through the Bible and prayer.
- Chooses to practice a variety of spiritual disciplines for training in godly character.
- Prioritizes time to nurture a deepening relationship with God.

# Day 1

## Be IN GOD'S WORD

John 15:1-8

*"I am the vine; you are the branches. Those who abide in me and I in them bear much fruit, because apart from me you can do nothing."* John 15:5 NRSV

## Be IN OUR STORY

"I have time for everything in my life—except me!" I cried. It was many years ago. I was suffering from a serious clinical depression. I had burned the candle, not only at both ends, but in the middle as well. I took care of my husband, child, house, work and church. Then, suddenly I found I couldn't take care of anything. That was hard to accept and I struggled with guilt, frustration and loss of control on top of everything else.

I had forgotten to take care of myself for so long, I had even forgotten how. I had forgotten to restore my physical being with plenty of sleep and quiet days, to replenish my spirit with God's love and to renew my mind with God's Word. I followed my own priorities, living on my own and in my own strength. I was a "branch" that forgot it needed to cling to the vine.

When I remembered to cultivate my walk with God and my own well-being, the outcome was that I had the time and strength for all. It's a mystery, isn't it? Jesus tells us to remain in him and we will do much, but apart from him, we can do nothing.

Remaining in him takes time—to pray, read the Word and meet with other believers. Our initial reaction to such a call is often "I don't have time for all that," but it is only in practicing these disciplines that we get time and strength for everything else—for without him, we can do nothing.

## *Be* IN THE QUESTIONS

1. What kind of branch are you—fallen, stand-alone, blossoming, leafless, laden with fruit?

2. No relationship can be developed by "osmosis." What practices help you to cultivate a deeper relationship with Christ?

3. In our busy lives, how can we ensure our walk with God is a priority?

## *Be* IN GOD'S PRESENCE

Lord, help me to remember to "remain" in you, to develop my relationship with you through prayer, reading the Bible and learning with other disciples of Christ. I know I can do nothing apart from you, but my actions don't reflect that some days. Help me to slow down and take the time to find out what you want my priorities to be, to join in what you are doing, rather than inventing my own list of things to do. Help me to make time to spend with you, so I have time and strength for everyone—including myself! Amen.

# Day 2

## *Be* IN GOD'S WORD

*Therefore, my dear friends, as you have always obeyed—not only in my presence, but now much more in my absence—continue to work out your salvation with fear and trembling, for it is God who works in you to will and to act according to his good purpose.*
Philippians 2:12-13

## *Be* IN OUR STORY

I held the baby in my arms, trying to get him to eat, even just a little. His body was limp, his mouth unmoving on the bottle, his staring eyes unable to meet my brokenhearted gaze. He had the worst case of a condition called "failure to thrive" of any child I had seen in my experience as a pediatric nurse.

I prayed for the child in my arms. "He is so beautiful, Lord, and his parents love him so much—his mom is beside herself with worry. Please Lord, let the doctors find out what is the underlying cause of his failure to thrive."

As I began to think about failure to thrive, I started to think about the number of people who have a spiritual version of the condition. They refuse to take in God's Word as food, they withdraw from the body of Christ, and their spiritual life slowly wastes away, as surely as the infant's life before me. Good food, love and support are essential factors in growth, but the child must respond and take it in, or it doesn't work. I think God would say, "So it is with me. I offer a personal relationship, I offer my children the Word for food, and the church body for support and love. If you refuse it, you too will waste away."

## *Be* IN THE QUESTIONS

1. Do you get your daily nutritional requirements from the Word of God?
2. Lack of proper nutrition and love in the first year of life can cause permanent, negative effects on a child's development. How can you take caution from this, and encourage the growth of a new believer?
3. God's Word says he will provide all we need—are you receiving it?

## *Be* IN GOD'S PRESENCE

Lord, I want to thrive spiritually, just like I want to improve my body through exercise and nutrition—but the truth is I am often unwilling to work long term at either! Help me to receive all the things you have provided for me. I want to be as committed to growing spiritually as I am about getting that workout in—and even more so! Help me to examine my condition when I experience spiritual failure to thrive to see if there is some underlying cause that could be repented of or remedied. I do love you Lord—help me to be more committed to love and live in you. Amen.

# Day 3

## *Be* IN GOD'S WORD

*For the word of God is living and active. Sharper than any double-edged sword, it penetrates even to dividing soul and spirit, joints and marrow; it judges the thoughts and attitudes of the heart.* Hebrews 4:12

*All scripture is inspired by God and is useful for teaching, for reproof, for correction, and for training in righteousness, so that everyone who belongs to God may be proficient, equipped for every good work.* II Timothy 3:16, 17

## *Be* IN OUR STORY

Do you ever find yourself reading a devotional book, and not getting into the Bible itself? I do. I too have heard all the sermons on the importance of reading the Word of God, but it became more of a reality one day when a leader in our church's adult ministry shared the following analogy:

> I am a celiac. This disease prevents me from eating wheat and other grains. What is a life-giving meal of pasta and bread for you would produce painful illness in me. I can eat rice bread—even though it tastes terrible—and it sustains my body. The bread you eat will not sustain me.
>
> And, just as we need to eat food daily, so we are sustained by eating God's Word each day. For the survival and good health of our spiritual bodies, we all need the living bread of God's Word. Like the manna God provided in the wilderness, God prepares a fresh, life-giving word for each of us each day.
>
> But, too often we put aside our Bibles and pick up books about the Bible instead. The problem with this is that these good books are something like the equivalent of stale bread—or bread given to someone else who has digested the bread and presented his or her offering from it. If this is our primary

diet, we will not be as spiritually healthy as when we read the Bible for ourselves daily, eating what God's Spirit has especially prepared for us.

Reading a devotional to make me think and reflect is good. Reading the Bible to get my "daily bread" prepared and served by the Living God—that's most important!

Feed on God's Word for you today – bon appetit!

*Personal story of Dave Swan*

## *Be* IN THE QUESTIONS

1. Extending the analogy of the Bible as the bread of life, how can we chew on, savor and digest God's Word?
2. How do you determine which part of God's Word to feed on each day?
3. How has God's Word fed you this week?

## *Be* IN GOD'S PRESENCE

Thank You Lord for your Word. Thank you that it is alive and given to each of us. Give me the desire to eat of it daily, to chew it over and allow it to be absorbed into my soul for my nourishment and growth. I appreciate the words of others, their thoughts and reflections, in which I see reflections of myself. What I really appreciate about the Bible is that it is your word to me, God, individually prepared to bring me life each day. Give me a good appetite! Amen.

# Day 4

## Be IN GOD'S WORD

II Peter 1:3-11

*His divine power has given us everything we need for life and godliness through our knowledge of him who called us by his own glory and goodness. For this reason, make every effort to add to your faith goodness; and to goodness, knowledge; and to knowledge, self-control; and to self-control, perseverance; and to perseverance, godliness; and to godliness, brotherly kindness; and to kindness, love. For if you possess these qualities in increasing measure, they will keep you from being ineffective and unproductive in your knowledge of our Lord Jesus Christ.* II Peter 1:3,5-8

## Be IN OUR STORY

Do you ever wish we could rub on a lotion to help us absorb everything we need to know? Or, even better, that we could insert a computer chip, push "run program" and find our character instantly changed? No struggle, no doubts, no fighting with God and self. Just "Presto, change-o!"

Sounds like fun, but it isn't how we learn. Learning takes work. Figuring out what to change and how to change also takes work, but the good news is that this part isn't all up to us! God sets the agenda of what needs to be changed. As we follow God's plans and will, we will be changed—he promises!

We follow God's plans and will through various activities which can be called spiritual disciplines. Just as my husband, the triathlete, must practice particular stretches and exercises to prepare for the race, watching his diet and sleep, so the Christian is given a series of recommended practices which will help him or her grow in the faith. Reading the Bible, prayer, memorizing Scripture, meditation, fasting, quiet retreats, joyful worship are all examples of spiritual disciplines.

There are many good books, and even some great ones, which teach us how to practice spiritual disciplines. There is one common factor in these guides: a disciple of Christ must DO IT! It isn't enough to know that we should do it, nor even to know how to do it—we need to actually do it, to stretch the muscles of our souls through spiritual disciplines.

And why do we do it? To gain heavenly brownie points? To determine how to fix ourselves? No. The right purpose for practicing spiritual disciplines is to communicate with God and to learn more about his heart and will. When we are communicating with God, change will happen. When we see ourselves in light of God's character, we will know what we need to learn or change, and will receive God's help in doing so.

Samuel heard God call his name, and responded *Speak Lord, for your servant is listening.* Moses took time to stop and consider the burning bush—and his life was never the same. Mary responded to God's call with immediate obedience and joy. Likewise God pursues us with call and love. Our job is not to figure out what to do, but to practice the disciplines which keep our hearts listening to God.

Do you want to do great things for God? Then keep the lines of communication with God open. Be willing to try out new spiritual exercises. Through regular listening to God, you will learn to know his character, recognize his voice and trust his heart. When God wants something done, you will be ready, willing and listening. Instead of practicing spiritual disciplines for "points," do them for the opportunity to be a point person for God here on earth.

## *Be* IN THE QUESTIONS

1. What is your usual motivation for praying, reading the Bible and having devotions?
2. Do you think change in your life has come more from your own initiative or God's? Which feels more forced? Which is most successful?
3. What difference would it make to your prayers if, instead of asking God to bless your plans, you asked to join in his plans?

## *Be* IN GOD'S PRESENCE

Dear God, I confess I often tell you all the things I want you to do. I often read Scripture so you will give me what I want and be pleased with me. Forgive me. Teach me to talk with you because we have a relationship. Help me to read your Word to learn more about who you are. Give me a growing desire for you, and help me to find satisfaction in pursuing you through the spiritual disciplines you have taught me. Thank you for pursuing me in love. Thank you that you change me because you love me and want me to become more like you. As I practice faithful acts, help me to do it only to draw me closer to you. Amen

# Day 5

## Be IN GOD'S WORD

*Walk in the way that the Lord your God has commanded you, so that you may live and prosper and prolong your days in the land that you will possess.* Deuteronomy 5:33

*As you therefore have received Christ Jesus the Lord, so walk in Him, rooted and built up in Him and established in the faith, as you have been taught, abounding in it with thanksgiving.*
Colossians 2:6,7 NKJV

## Be IN OUR STORY

I am so shortsighted that the last time I visited the optometrist, she told me if my eyes got any worse, she would strap binoculars to my head! If I take my glasses off, I can only see what is in front of my nose—literally. But when I put my glasses on, my vision is restored and I can see a long way. That is what I have to do every-day with my eyeglasses, but also with my spiritual vision. Sometimes when I don't have time for God or I'm going through a tough time, it helps to force myself to put on "spiritual glasses," to gain an eternal perspective on my life. It amazes me how long I can go around fumbling my way through life before I stop and retreat with God. Even a short time with God and his word can restore my spiritual sight. It's astonishing how quickly God meets me there, offering me his eyes—eternal vision—to look at my life and our world.

So why do I struggle to do it? Why do I run away from God when I'm hurt or afraid or angry? Why don't I hold out my hand to ask for help? On my fridge, I have a quote: "Practice in the dark what you learned in the light." Sometimes, I confess, I have to read this quote a dozen times before I will finally go to God. What seems real and makes sense in the light, seems uncertain and scary in the dark. My vision can be darkened and what I need is to spend time with God, waiting on him until I am reassured. Sometimes what is needed is a long time of prayer. Often I read the Bible, reminding myself of all the great things God has done. Other times, I read old journals or count my blessings. These are reminders, "forget me nots" of the faith. Forcing myself beyond my feelings to do in the dark what I learned in the light restores my spiritual vision with eternal perspective of our faithful God.

## *Be* IN THE QUESTIONS

1. What helps restore your spiritual vision? When was the last time you did it?
2. What makes you turn a cold shoulder to God? What do you need to remember or learn about his character to help you turn to him?
3. Is there a situation in your life today which needs to recapture an eternal perspective? Do it!

## *Be* IN GOD'S PRESENCE

Lord, I thank you for your patience with me. You are so willing to give wisdom and strength for life's challenges, and yet when I need them most, I run! How foolish it seems after the fact. Thank you that when I do look up to you, instead of focusing on the here and now realities, you answer. You don't always take the problems away, but you walk with me, helping me to remember life in terms of eternity. You are beautiful and faithful Lord—even I can see that. Amen.

# Weekend stories

## GOD'S DOG

I have noticed lately that God is treating me like I treat my dog—oh, it isn't his fault, it's mine. I just seem to be so busy that I read one quick verse and fly out the door—and that's when I hear him: "Sit! Stay!" He means it kindly, I'm sure. He never barks at me in irritation. And it makes me wish that I were, metaphorically speaking, God's dog. I want to be the kind that heels correctly and obediently when asked, that willingly follows the Master around, watching his every move so I would know where to go. My usual self pulls as God tries to lead, runs off in my own direction, barking at God to follow me. I would like to be the kind of dog that gets so excited by the sight of his Master, that lays contentedly by his feet, listening attentively to all he says. I would like to be the kind of dog that looks attentively for my Master when we have to be apart. Actually, I would like to apply all those "good dog" qualities to my life as a person. With my dog, obedience begins when he follows my command to sit and stay, and the same is likely true for God's dog —I mean, person) too. The next time he asks, I will obey. Maybe this old dog could learn some new tricks after all.

••••••••••••••••••••••••••••••••

## DEEP ROOTS

I am only an amateur gardener—but I am an avid one. Wandering through garden stores, choosing just the right plants, is a soothing activity for my soul. One day, after a project I had worked on for two years fell through, I turned to my garden, and soon found myself heading off to my favorite plant store for some soul healing and to finish off a spot in my garden. I found the perfect plant covered with closed buds that were ready to open as soon as I tenderly planted it. I had visions of how beautiful this plant would look in my garden. As I paid for my prize plant, the cashier advised me about planting: she said I needed to cut off the top third of the plant so its roots would grow deep and the plant would come back healthier, more able to withstand the heat and drought of summer. She explained that hothouse plants were so rushed to grow their roots weren't yet strong enough to support the growth. I was stunned. Had I heard her right? Cut off the beautiful buds?

I felt like an executioner. I dug the hole, placed the plant carefully in the ground, and added fertilizer and water. Then I stood and weighed the cashier's words. Cut it off just as it is about to bloom? What if it just withers and dies? Or will it be better in the long run? She had better be right about this. With trembling hands and cutters, I chopped. Then, I turned from my unsightly plant and walked into the house.

Over the next few weeks, a few people questioned my taste in plants, but sure enough, eventually even more buds began to appear and the plant grew heartily, lasting all summer, despite the heat and my fitful watering.

I am reminded of my daughter's grade four project on deserts. I remember that desert plants adapt to the heat, by sending very deep roots into the ground to deep underground water sources. I recall that cactuses store water when it rains and live on the stored water when it gets dry.

Some plants need to be pruned in order to develop those deep roots, even though pruning looks—and feels—like the last thing you should be doing. God wants me to develop those kinds of roots too—roots which reach out to him for life giving water, roots which allow me to thrive in the driest of times. When God prunes me, it may hurt and it may look like my little stick of a plant, but he does it to make me fruitful and spiritually beautiful. I'll remember that each time I look at my garden.

••••••••••••••••••••

## DEAR SON,

It was so good to talk with you last week. I'm glad you are enjoying your new house. I was proud to learn that you are now starting to think about looking for someone you can love. I have had the good fortune to fall in love, and in fact, each day I am falling more and more in love. The object of my love is our Lord. I want to share a secret with you on how I am starting to discover God in a very new way.

The way I fell in love was through prayer, where I discovered God, my loving Father. The apostles asked Jesus, *Lord, teach us to pray* (Luke 11:1) and for years, I read this request and skimmed right over it, without realizing what it meant. Sure, I knew consistent prayer was important—how else do we get out of problems? Nevertheless, I did not find communing with God as easy as some books claim, until recently, and now I enjoy talking with the Lord more and more.

Your Grandpa taught me that the proper position for prayer was on my knees, asking the Lord for help. This pose is very official and it might be true, but I have also come to learn other things about prayer. First, I have discovered that some of my best prayers happen when I am dangling headfirst off a roof, with nothing left to do but pray! However, more importantly, I have learned that I don't need to have a dilemma to talk to our Father.

I am spending more time just hanging out with the Father than actually asking for help. We all pray when we're desperate—just as we all eat when we're hungry—but hanging out with God is a different matter. Your old Dad is hanging out with God and that is the secret of falling in love.

Have you ever tried praying in your car, in the shower, or while jogging (don't worry—I'm not taking up jogging again!)? Lots of Christians pray in the morning before starting the day, but have you ever prayed in the supermarket while waiting your turn to pay? Last week, I caught myself praying while cutting my grass—telling God how pleased I was that you had bought a house and were enjoying your job.

I have found lately that the more I pray, the more I want to pray. It's funny—something I sweated over, I now desire. Prayer is not so much a technique as an approach to life. Son, prayer has brought me to the point where I recognize that God is the Lord, and I belong to him, and I wanted to share this discovery with someone I love very much.

All the best, stay out of deep water, and remember that God answers prayers.

Dad

*Story by D. Swan*

••••••••••••••••••••••••••••••••••

# BONDED AND BUILDING

**Scriptures:**

Acts 2:38-47; Hebrews 10:19-25; I Corinthians 12:7-27

**God's Initiative:**

*And now God is building you, as living stones, into his spiritual temple...who offer the spiritual sacrifices that please him because of Jesus Christ.* 1 Peter 2:5

**Description:**

A person who engages with a community of faith, in small group and larger contexts, and develops as a contributor to the health and effectiveness of a local congregation.

**Evidence:**

- Learns to live the Christian life in community with other believers, giving and receiving a maturing level of discipling, accountability and support.
- Displays an unfolding awareness of a unique identity in Christ and joyfully uses spiritual gifts to serve.
- Practices generosity with time and resources.

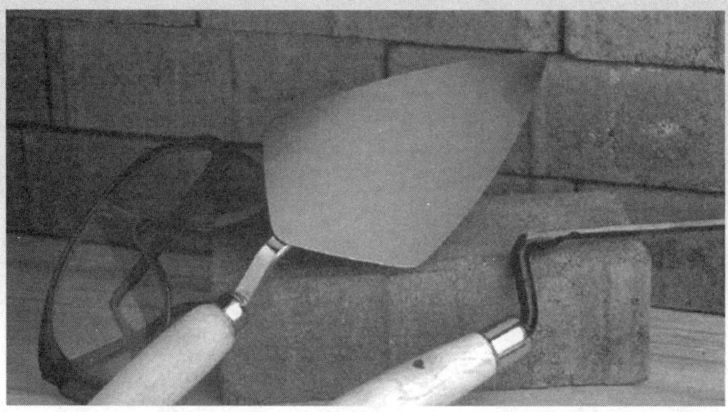

# Day 1

## Be IN GOD'S WORD

Hebrews 10:19-25

*Let us not give up meeting together, as some are in the habit of doing, but let us encourage each other—and all the more as you see the Day approaching.* Hebrews 10:25

## Be IN OUR STORY

There is an old saying: It's hard to fly like an eagle when you have to work with turkeys. That particular expression often comes to mind when I'm struggling to work with others in the church. Many people claim to believe in God, but not the church—the people they meet there get in the way of their spirituality. I've had my days where I sympathize with this view—the morning after a church meeting where every idea I proposed got dumped with cold water, the time I felt stabbed in the back by a fellow believer. Those days I wonder why I bother with the church.

God calls us to fellowship with other Christians so we might encourage one another. I also suspect that it is so our real character can be exposed. It is far easier to be God-centered and act righteously when I am alone. It's when I have to interact with other people—family, friends and fellow church members—that my faith meets the road. I confess it often goes "splat!" Sometimes I even realize that I'm the turkey in the way of the other eagles.

Servanthood, giving ourselves for the sake of others, is the essence of discipleship. But, too often we church members don't treat each other like we are members of the same body (I Corinthians 12), let alone giving ourselves for the sake of each other.

I have had some of my toughest life lessons from those who professed their friendship and caring to me, walking together as fellow believers. One particular day, I was so upset by how another believer had treated me I lay at the front of the church sobbing. I started by telling God how hurt I was and then began dumping my anger about the situation at him. "Do you have any idea how betrayed I feel? Do you know how this feels to be treated like this? They said they cared about me and then they just walk away once they have what they want." I cried until I could cry no more. Then, as I got up, my eyes suddenly caught the cross, and as I was finally quiet enough to listen, I heard the Lord say, "Yes, I know exactly how it feels to be betrayed—to be loved, then deceived and disowned. I know all too well what it feels like, so come let us hold one another." I sat quietly, talking to the Lord. We agreed that people can be harsh, mean and cruel and that it is hard to take. Then Jesus asked me to lay my pain and grief at the cross before him so God could make good come out of this evil, as he had done for Jesus. I have never had such an intimate moment with Jesus—all the teaching about Jesus as a man who suffered suddenly moved from my head to my heart—and I began the slow process of letting go and becoming whole.

Being part of a church is not always easy, but *God has arranged the parts of the body, every one of them, just as he wanted them to be* (I Corinthians 12:18). Our task is to learn to live the Christian life in community, to encourage one another and to bring our concerns about the church to God in prayer. When we learn to do this, there is nothing more beautiful. The church is also called the bride of Christ, and when the church works together in unity and love, we have glimpses of heavenly glory and joy.

## *Be* IN THE QUESTIONS

1. Is it other believers who annoy you or the fact that your true self comes out around them?
2. I Corinthians 8 teaches us to be careful not to make another believer stumble. Verse 11 says that this *weak brother, for whom Christ died, is destroyed by your knowledge.* The next time you are furious with another believer, remember that Christ died for both of you before you approach the problem.
3. What are the joys you have experienced by being part of a local church?

## *Be* IN GOD'S PRESENCE

Lord, I'm glad to be one of your disciples, but I confess that sometimes the other disciples make it hard. Help me to remember that none of us are perfect and that we all need you. Help me to put my experiences of pain in light of yours. Help me to see others as you do—as people you love and died for—and to build them up with encouragement. Help us together to become your beautiful, loving bride. Amen.

# Day 2

## Be IN GOD'S WORD

I Corinthians 12:7-27

*Now you are the body of Christ, and each one of you is a part of it.*
I Corinthians 12:27

## Be IN OUR STORY

From the corner of my eye I see the puzzle go flying across the room.

"What are you doing?" I ask my six year old daughter.

"The dumb puzzle I got is broken!" she retorts.

"It isn't broken, a puzzle comes in pieces. You are supposed to put it together." I try to keep the giggle out of my voice.

"That's not what I mean! I want this piece to fit here and it won't!"

"That's not how it works. You have to look carefully at the pieces, see what matches and try them in different places until they fit."

"Where are the scissors?" she asks. "I'll fix it properly!"

"You can't fix or force it. You have to find out where it belongs."

"But it's one of those mystery puzzles with no picture on the box. If I can't see the whole picture, how can I put it together?"

"Well, that will take more time but don't give up! See if you can find a pattern among the pieces themselves. Put certain parts together so you can see if they make the shape of something. You are so good at puzzles. Sit back and look at the pieces. What do you see in the little pieces by themselves? Do you recognize anything?"

"Yes," she says hesitantly, holding up a few pieces. " I guess I can see some things, but it isn't really clear."

"It won't be at first, but as you go along, things will become clearer and will begin to fit easier. You may not see the details or even the whole picture until you are almost done but you will begin to see the overall design."

"How can I know where this piece should go?"

"Usually you are looking for a piece that is exactly opposite. So if your piece has an end that sticks out, match it to a piece that has an indented curve in it, then they will make a good fit as each piece gives the other one the part it is missing."

"Once all the pieces are together it will make a cool design, won't it?" Hope and excitement come back into her voice.

"I bet it will be something you couldn't have even imagined!"

## *Be* IN THE QUESTIONS

1. Why do we hope that if we "throw" our gifts and abilities together that all the pieces will fit together nicely and easily? What happens to people when the church forces them into positions?
2. Why is it a good idea to not just stick with "pieces" like us? How do we (and the church) benefit when we work with and befriend people who are different from us?
3. Although only God knows the complete picture of our service to him, we can get a sense of the overall design as we examine our spiritual gifts, our talents, our personality and our experiences to see where we can offer service to the church. What patterns do you see God building in you? How does this help you see where you can fit into your local church?

## *Be* IN GOD'S PRESENCE

Lord, you see the full picture of my life. Help me to discover my spiritual gifts with as much enthusiasm as I have when I open Christmas presents. Help me to take the talents you have given me and multiply them for your glory. Whether I am the quiet type or have great charisma, help me to keep in mind that you can use my personality to express my gifts in ministry and service, that my personality is not the hindrance of my service, but the how. Thank you for making me a wonderful puzzle in your image. Give me the grace to be patient enough, with myself and others, to fit it all together. Amen.

# Day 3

## Be IN GOD'S WORD

Acts 2: 38-47

*They devoted themselves to the apostles' teaching and to fellowship, to the breaking of bread and prayer. Selling their possessions and goods, they gave to anyone as he had need. Every day they continued to meet together in the temple courts. They broke bread in their homes and ate together with glad and sincere hearts, praising God and enjoying the favor of all the people. And the Lord added to their number daily those who were being saved.*
Acts 2:42, 45-47

## Be IN OUR STORY

I opened the paper and scanned the headline: "It Takes a Village." This time it was the title of a review of a children's book; another day it was used to promote access to daycare. But, though the phrase is overused to the point of cliché, the idea has been around a long time—in fact, the early church modeled it. We've just forgotten its truth in our generation of distances separating families and the "go it alone" mentality.

The original African proverb means that in a village, a family nurtures and loves each child, with a close group of accountability and support for both child and parents, as well as a larger group—the "village"—which also participates in the development of various aspects of the child.

I decide to write an article about this concept within the Christian church—how when you become a Christian and join the family of believers, you are now part of the village. The church offers you a place to learn and fellowship and become a part of the "big picture." Within this group your gifts and talents can be recognized and developed. You also need to be part of a small group of people who will encourage you, hold you accountable and carry you when you can't make it on your own. Though needing help is seen as weak in our culture, in the Christian village, the journey involves helping each other along the way. You can also live out your faith within your family, whether they believe or not. If they do, they can nurture your walk with God, but if they do not, the "village" becomes all the more important.

Thinking about families reminds me of the memo on my fridge on which I have printed some responsibilities of family:

> When we raise you to have a strong, solid faith in God; to be self aware, yet God reliant, in who you are and what you can do; to be consistently thoughtful toward others yet knowing your own thoughts; to be able to give and receive help along life's journey...our job, for the most part, is done!

These are also worthy goals in how we nurture each other in our church "village."

I want to include all these thoughts in my article, but I struggle to make the ideas practical. Then the phone rings. It's a friend whose family always acted as though her faith was useless until she landed a great job with a Christian organization. Now they are treating her differently, introducing her with pride. While she's glad, she's hurt too. We talk about families and hurts and then suddenly I am reminded of the "village" concept. I tell her that maybe her family doesn't think that highly of her walk with God but her "village" sure does. I get off the phone and praise the Lord for helping someone through my work. Isn't that just like God to go before us and prepare the way?

## *Be* IN THE QUESTIONS

1. How has the church "village" supported you?
2. Galatians 6:2 tells us to bear each other's burdens and so fulfill the law of Christ. At times we lack strength, but when we share our concerns with others, they can help carry us. How can a small group help someone through a time of difficulty? How can a small group celebrate with someone who is rejoicing? What have you been through that could help others in your small group?
3. Re-read the opening Scripture verses. Acts 2: 45—*they gave to anyone who had need*—jumped off the page for me. I don't know if I have even been looking around lately to see who in my village is in need. Have you?

## *Be* IN GOD'S PRESENCE

Lord, what a privilege to be a part of your village. What a blessing to have others hold us up when our faith is shaking or our world is quaking. Thank you for providing people around us to help us mature and "grow up" in our faith. Help us to become adults in our faith, loving you, serving you and representing you! Amen.

# Day 4

## Be IN GOD'S WORD

Matthew 22:16 – 22

*And He said to them, "Render therefore to Caesar the things that are Caesar's, and to God the things that are God's."*
Matthew 22: 21 NJKV

## Be IN OUR STORY

Have you ever really thought about these verses? I confess I looked at them in the usual way—paying taxes and tithing—until I read an article called "Give to God What is God's."[1] The author of this article claimed more was at stake than just money.

Giving our resources of time and money to God is not only important—it is commanded of us. The Old Testament model of giving a minimum of ten percent of our harvest is a clear command: *A tithe of everything from the land…belongs to the Lord; it is holy to the Lord* (Leviticus 27:30). Jesus teaches the equal importance of good stewardship of our time: *Seek first the kingdom of God and his righteousness* (Matthew 6:33).

But still, the article explained, there was more going on. So what else was Jesus talking about here? Jesus said we were to give to the government what it was owed and to give to God the things that were his. But if the coin was to go to Caesar because of the image it bore, then likewise anything bearing God's image should go to him. What bears God's image? Us! God created people in his image. We carry his image "stamped" on us just like a coin. I had never thought of stewardship that way! We, of course, have free will and so we can choose to live our life as we want or as one who bears the image of God.

When we recognize we are stamped with God's image, we express our stewardship by giving back to God a share of our money, time and other resources. But, we also can express our stewardship by giving ourselves for work in the local church, in the world —wherever God calls us to go.

From this perspective, stewardship is exciting. We can participate in what God is doing in his world and in our lives, by offering ourselves and all we have to his wonderful purposes.

## *Be* IN THE QUESTIONS

1. We often grudgingly give our tithe. What will change your attitude about giving of yourselves and your resources?
2. How do you determine how to give your time, money and other resources to God's work? Which of these needs attention right now?
3. As you take to heart the fact that you bear the image of God, how does it change your perspective of yourself? How does it change your perspective of giving of yourself to God's purposes?

## *Be* IN GOD'S PRESENCE

How incredible to be reminded that we bear the image of God! They say the longer people live together, the more alike they become. Lord, I pray that this will be true of my relationship with you. May I become more and more a reflection of you! When I sit in your presence and think on the wonder of this relationship with you, giving my money, resources and even my very self seem like such meager offerings to show how much I love you. What you gave me, your Son, now that was love! What an honor to be a child, servant, friend and even a reflection of God himself. Amen.

1. "Give to God What is God's" by Rawlin and Pam Falk. The Path of the Righteous. September 2003.

## *Be* IN GOD'S WORD

*For by the grace given me I say to every one of you: Do not think of yourself more highly than you ought, but rather think of yourself with sober judgment, in accordance with the measure of faith God has given you. Just as each of us has one body with many members, and these members do not all have the same function, so in Christ we who are many form one body, and each member belongs to all the others. We have different gifts, according to the grace given us.* Romans 12: 3-6

## *Be* IN OUR STORY

When God called Nehemiah to rebuild the wall of Jerusalem, Nehemiah had to gather many people from the small Israelite community to help. This project became one of spiritual guidance and growth as well as physical reconstruction. All the various families were assigned to different sections of the wall. People contributed to the project in different ways, from builders to guards, so that the project would be completed. Did it all go well? In the end, yes, but it was not easy. Many obstacles came up, opportunists took advantage of others and some tried to undermine the work. Prayer, accountability, confrontation and working together in humble unity got the job done. The result? *So the wall was finished... when all our enemies heard of it, and all the nations around us saw these things, that they were very disheartened in their own eyes; for they perceived that this work was done by our God* (Nehemiah 6:15-16 NKJV).

A practical application for our churches? It takes all of us to build what God has called us to. Those who are more mature or experienced are to teach and help others learn the way. We are all to help each other, to encourage each other and keep each other accountable. As we focus on the work God gives us, praying and seeking God, then God's enemies will be *disheartened in their own eyes; for they perceived that this work was done by our God.*

A practical application for us individually? Our gifts, talents and just plain hard work are needed. It takes all of us—not just the leaders. A leader's job is to show the vision God has given and to lead the way, but it is everyone's job to make it a reality. We all must work and kneel together, regardless of our differences, keeping our eye on the "goal" and remembering it is not work done by people, but *this work was done by our God*. How exciting to be a part of it!

## *Be* IN THE QUESTIONS

1. What is your role in building up the church? Think in terms of functions but also in terms of relationships.
2. The nursery rhyme "Jack Spratt" teaches us that we need different types of people to "lick the platter clean." How do our differences help us to serve God together? What is the difference between "oneness" and "sameness"?
3. How are you contributing to the health and effectiveness of your church and how are you a hindrance to its growth and well-being?

## *Be* IN GOD'S PRESENCE

Lord, help me to remember that all of us are important in the work you call us to. You have made us all differently so we can complete the works you ask of the church. Help us to celebrate our oneness and not focus on our lack of sameness. Thank you for examples of strong leaders like Nehemiah and the Israelites who did your work—what started as the building of a wall became a revival and return of your people to you. May we be so blessed to be a part of such works in our own time, Lord. Amen.

# *Weekend stories*

## CONNECTING

She looked at the floor, shoulders slumped, unsmiling. I tried to engage her in the conversation without putting her on the spot.

I was teaching a class on how God uses us for his service. We had covered spiritual gifts, talents, personality and life experiences, and now we were discussing how God often uses our passions, the things we love to do. She was silent as others shared their passions and dreams. I quietly prayed and then felt compelled to be direct. "What about you?" I asked, finally catching her eye. "What do you love to do?"

"God couldn't use what I like to do," she replied. "My favorite thing is to talk on the phone. I have small kids and it is the only way I get adult conversation. I don't have time to be in ministry, so whatever I can do for God will have to wait." Another person then asked, "And how could God use my love for shopping?"

("Triumph!" my spirit shouted.)

"Well," I said to the first woman. " You said your spiritual gift was encouragement, right? And you love to talk on the phone. So what about using your passion and your gifts to have a 'phone encouragement' ministry? Go through the church directory asking God to show you someone who needs encouragement, then call them. Now you are blessing others and doing it through something you love and can do with small kids. Ministry doesn't have to wait—and now you'll have a reason to be on the phone, a God given one!" We all laughed and for the first time all class she smiled.

I turned to the shopping lover. "What about going to a community support agency and volunteering as a shopping assistant for the elderly? You get to be part of the community, do what you like and serve God all in one."

"I've never thought of my love for shopping as a help to others," she replied, smiling. "I'd love to do that."

God can use all aspects of us any time, anywhere and in many, even unusual, ways as we turn our gifts and passions over to his purposes.

••••••••••••••••••••••••••••••••

## CONSIDERING COVENANT CAREFULLY

"Hold up your end of the relationship!" the pastor said. "You come here to be fed and encouraged, but what do you do to contribute to that?" *Boy, we're a quiet crowd.*

"Jesus began the church so we can learn to dwell together. What do you think we will do when we get to heaven—live in separate universes? Look around you; these are the people you will be in heaven with. So if you hope they might move away soon, surprise, you'll see them again!" *I look over to my left and my heart sinks.*

"Why the church? Surely there must be an easier way? We all ask that at times. I could be a great Christian if it weren't for those around me who make me so frustrated. The truth is nothing can come out of you that wasn't already there." *Did anyone else hear that pin drop?*

"If you can't come to church and make a covenant to stay here, be a member and work through things for your faith—through is the operative word—then how do you expect to last in your covenant with God?" *Hmmmm...*

"We don't take covenants very seriously anymore. We make a covenant to a spouse and then leave when it becomes work. We make a covenant of membership to a church and leave when we are offended and it becomes work. Do we also, in some ways, make a covenant with God to be a follower of Christ and then...leave when it takes work?" *Is it just me or are these pews extra uncomfortable today?*

"Even Jesus said we should consider a covenant with him carefully. Read Luke 9:57-62 or Luke 14:25-35 to learn the cost of being a disciple. Jesus tells people to think it through, to count the cost BEFORE making the commitment. Following Jesus means giving up our attachments to things and people. Putting God first in all things is what it means to be a disciple. We sell Christianity today as a 'haven from life's problems, a place to get it all here on earth, as an escape from hell', but that is not what the Bible teaches. For some people, covenant with Christ means losing our jobs, being disowned by our friends and family. How many of us in this warm, beautiful church would follow Christ if that is what it meant? How many of us here would say yes to Christ if it meant death? How many of us would even show up if we had to walk miles to get here or stand for hours to hear the word? Or if we had to decide whether to eat today or pay to catch the bus to come to church?" *My new shoes are pinching my toes—walk how far, did he say?*

"Christ invites you. But count the cost. Be sure of the commitment. Then come on the journey with us." *I will take some time in the closing moments of the service to reflect and pray and I choose to follow.*

•••••••••••••••••••••••••••••••••

# INVITING AND INFLUENCING

**Scriptures:**

Matthew 28:19-20; 2 Corinthians 5:11-21; Luke 19:1-9

**God's Initiative:**

*No one can come to me unless the Father...draws him.* John 6:44

**Description:**

A person who develops an invitational lifestyle in everyday relationships, contagiously attracting others toward Christ.

**Evidence:**

- Knows the importance of sharing faith and how to introduce a person to Christ.
- Learns to pray for and relate redemptively to non-Christian peers.
- Becomes a compassionate witness, demonstrating Christ's love by meeting practical needs and enthusiastically participating in group efforts to draw others to Christ.

# Day 1

## Be IN GOD'S WORD

*"Therefore go and make disciples of all nations, baptizing them in the name of the Father and of the Son and of the Holy Spirit, and teaching them to obey everything I have commanded you. And surely I am with you always, to the very end of the age."*
Matthew 28:19-20

## Be IN OUR STORY

The missionary is here from some far away place. He drones on. He shows slides. I am bored. I am glad I wasn't called to be a missionary. I could not do what he does: all that filth, being an outsider, the harshness and danger. I am comfortable here in my nice, safe neighborhood. The yards are well kept. The people are friendly. The garbage and mail service are great. I can come to church with other believers and sit in safety to hear yet another sermon.

But I begin to feel uncomfortable. He seems to shine with excitement as he talks about what Jesus is doing there. I am not sure what Jesus is doing around here. The missionary seems so content in the midst of that hardship. I have a far better life and I am not content. What does he know that I do not? What has he applied to his life that I have not applied to mine? What have I forgotten that he dwells on each day as he serves with gladness? My spirit is awakened within me to find answers to these questions.

The missionary has come to tell us about the great work Jesus is doing overseas, but the missionary began a great work here today as well.

## *Be* IN THE QUESTIONS

1. "Go and tell" is such a simple phrase, so why do we struggle to do it?

2. Why is it so hard to tell others about being obedient to the word of God? Is it that we think we are poor examples? What should we do if this guilt is real? What if it's false?

3. What is Jesus doing around you? How can you join in?

## *Be* IN GOD'S PRESENCE

Lord, help me to remember that I am in your service, right here everyday, wherever I go. I desire to deepen my relationship with you that your love might shine through me. Help me to grow in love for the lost, as I once was lost too. I want to see the world as you see it. May my life reflect that which I proclaim to believe. And most of all help me to look around for you and see what you are doing here, where I am. Could I please be a part of that? Thank you! Amen.

# Day 2

## Be IN GOD'S WORD

2 Corinthians 5: 11-21

*So from now on we regard no one from a worldly point of view. Though we once regarded Christ in this way, we do so no longer. Therefore, if anyone is in Christ, he is a new creation; the old has gone, the new has come! We are therefore Christ's ambassadors, as though God were making his appeal through us.*
2 Corinthians 5:16, 17, 20a

## Be IN OUR STORY

We were on vacation at my parent's place at Kootenay Lake, B.C., and we stopped at a glass blowing shop in a nearby town. Each piece the owner had made was absolutely breath taking. There were all kinds of shapes, sizes and colors. Twirling and swirling, some melted into the most daring designs while others were of the subtlest nature. I was so amazed at their beauty and attractiveness, I could hardly decide which was my favorite. I held one exceptional vase in my hand and wanted to take it home. "Imagine this with flowers in it," I said to my husband. He was amazed at the craftsmanship and how the heating, stretching and pulling transformed a blob of useless glass into a work of art which was also a useful object.

I began wishing I were like the vase—bright, beautiful, no flaws! Think of all the people I would attract to God if I could be like this vase. As soon as we got home I showed the vase to my mother. Later as we sat outside sipping ice tea, I told my Mom how I wished I was like the vase. She just smiled and we sat silently. A minute later she asked me how I liked her potted plants in front of the house. "They are gorgeous," I said, "I noticed them as soon as we drove up. I would love to get a clump for my garden."

"Mmmmm," my mom replied. "That's what everyone says. But you know, they're planted in an ordinary pot, a bit broken on the side, all marked up from being banged around." She paused and looked me in the eye. "Funny thing," she said, "no one ever notices my pot. They see what's inside, and they always want some." She quietly walked into the house while I pondered her words of wisdom.

## *Be* IN THE QUESTIONS

1. How much of yourself do you reflect? How much of God?
2. Is it hard to accept being an "ordinary pot"? What is the blessing in being ordinary?
3. When we let God shine through us, how does it become easier to lead people toward reconciliation with God?

## *Be* IN GOD'S PRESENCE

Lord, I have a secret: I want to be a shiny pot. I don't always admit it out loud, but I do. I see lots of other shiny pots around me and I am attracted to them. But actually as I think about it, I don't even look to see what is inside those shiny pots, since I am so taken with their dazzle. Maybe that's why you use ordinary pots. You want us to remember we may be ordinary on the outside but inside, as you renew and change us with your love, we become new—shining out God's message of reconciliation—instead of the shiny message of "be like me." Today I will remember the joy of being an ordinary pot, and let you, God, be on display. Amen.

# Day 3

## *Be* IN GOD'S WORD

Luke 19: 1-9

*Jesus entered Jericho...A man was there by the name of Zacchaeus...He wanted to see who Jesus was...so he ran ahead and climbed a sycamore-fig tree to see him...When Jesus reached the spot he looked up and said to him, "Zacchaeus, come down immediately. I must stay at your house today." ...Jesus said to him, "Today salvation has come to this house...For the Son of Man came to seek and to save what was lost."* Luke 19: 1-5, 9

## *Be* IN OUR STORY

I know the story of Zacchaeus well. But it troubles me. It reminds me how often I make a point of not getting to know non-Christians. It bothers me because when I take a long hard look, I am forced to realize I often act as though such people might "tarnish" me in some way. I would never say this out loud to anyone, but when I look at my actions, I wonder what I do believe about people outside the faith.

Zaccheus also troubles me because when Jesus went to be with the sinner, he "brought salvation to the house." Too often, I bring nothing but talk about myself. Often I go away having been more affected by their lives than having had any effect on theirs.

Sometimes it is hard to read the story of Zacchaeus. At least not without realizing I have sin to confess and I need to follow Jesus' example. There is a lot of work to do in reaching the lost, and it starts with realizing my need to examine my own heart.

## *Be* IN THE QUESTIONS

1. Jesus made such an impact on the world that sinful people like Zaccheus sought him out to see for themselves. What kind of impact do you make on the world around you—or do you just blend in?
2. Jesus brought salvation to the house he visited; what do you bring?
3. To what extent do we need to be concerned about being effected by non-Christians, and in what ways is this an excuse for fear?

## *Be* IN GOD'S PRESENCE

Lord, I have read and re-read some of these Bible stories. Perhaps the problem is that I read them as stories, not as truth. When I read to learn, I begin to see the example you set and am led to reflect on my own heart and actions. Ouch! It is often painful. I come on bended knee to confess my own sins—my pride and fear, my desire to stay comfortable and keep your love to myself. Please forgive me so I might run out and share willingly with others what I have experienced from God. Help me to seek out those you love and to tell them of the incredible gift you offer them and me, *all of us sinners*, whom you love so much that you have pursued us since the beginning of time. Amen.

## *Be* IN GOD'S WORD

I Corinthians 1:26-31

*Let the one who boasts, boast in the Lord.* I Corinthians 1:31 NRSV

## *Be* IN OUR STORY

In my first two years at university, I had stood strong in my walk with God. I said "no" to the pub nights, the risqué movies, and wild dorm parties. I was involved in sports. Athletics provided an opportunity to develop some very special friendships as we spent many hours training together. During that time there were opportunities to share one's thoughts and beliefs. One friend in particular seemed to be interested in my belief in God. Our talks deepened and our friendship grew. This friendship provided reason for me to be more diligent in my Christian walk and testimonial of God's love. How thrilling it would be, I thought, if she could come to know Christ as her personal Savior and friend. I strived to be the "perfect" Christian so she would see God.

But in my third year of university, I found myself struggling with hurts and scars of a childhood ravaged by abuse. The pain and confusion led to despair and an abandonment of my Christian walk. I felt I had failed God, my friends and myself. What chance did any of them have now to make a choice to follow the "life of Christ"? I had blown all of that. I was a hypocrite, a phoney. How could I ever make things right again? As the year passed, I slowly regained my step and found myself clinging to God for strength. Would my friends understand that God forgives and welcomes back someone like me? I wasn't sure. I left the university that spring exhausted and discouraged. Maybe a summer away would erase the mistakes.

Early that summer I received a phone call from my special friend. She was wondering if she could come and stay with me for a few days—she had something she wanted to share with me. On a warm, sunny day at a baseball park, my friend shared with me that she had accepted Jesus as her Savior and friend. I wept tears of joy, yet I also felt sorrowful, knowing I had had no part in her coming to know Jesus. I asked her what influenced her to make that decision. She began to tell me how for three years she watched me, asking questions and listening. What she heard and saw in the first two years of our friendship made her think that she was not worthy to belong to God. Her life was full of too many "wrong" choices. It wasn't until she saw me stumble and fall in my walk with God that she realized God would accept her too. I seemed to be more "human." I'll never forget that moment—I was in awe! How could God possibly have used me—a failure, weak, and broken? And yet He did—and my friend became my sister in Christ.

*Personal testimony of Jan Kroeker*

## *Be* IN THE QUESTIONS

1. How do we live in such a way that people are drawn toward Christ? Can we believe that our weaknesses as well as our strengths speak to people?
2. In what relationships today am I consciously modeling my relationship with Christ as an invitation to others to know him?
3. What do we do when we "blow it"?

## *Be* IN GOD'S PRESENCE

Lord, I am constantly amazed at how you use weak and broken vessels. You show me that you don't require me to be perfect before you can use me. In fact, your power is made perfect through my weakness. Then there is no doubt that it is you shining through me. Thank you that I can relax, be myself—your child enjoying our friendship together—and that I can introduce my other friends to you. Show me those who are eager to know you. Amen.

# Day 5

## *Be* IN GOD'S WORD

2 Corinthians 5: 11-21

*All this is from God, who reconciled us to himself through Christ and gave us the ministry of reconciliation: that God was reconciling the world to himself in Christ, not counting men's sins against them. And he has committed to us the message of reconciliation.*
2 Corinthians 5: 18 – 19

## *Be* IN OUR STORY

If we look perfect, how will anyone realize Christ's redemptive power? If we expect the world to "have their act together" before they come to church, why come? And if perfection is the criteria, what are we doing there?

I became keenly aware that I was so busy trying to get my act together before sharing Christ with someone that the sharing never happened! Now, I am trying a different approach: I make a friend. I'm me—with good points and bad, with struggles and triumphs. But in the midst of it all I share Christ—not Carol—Christ. What a difference! Any power is Christ's, not mine.

Jesus committed the message of reconciliation to each of us believers. This is the same message we needed and received. I tend to forget that it is my sin that put Jesus on the cross, every bit as much as the sin of my non-Christian neighbor. Too often I hold my head up in pride and righteousness, instead of recalling in humility that Jesus took on my sin so I could be reconciled to God. I need to remember to be awestruck that it was God who loved me first, instead of thinking how lucky God is to have me love him. I need to willingly give the message of reconciliation that I so eagerly received and still need every day! If I recall how blessed I am to have received the message, what am I doing standing here keeping it to myself? In Paul's words, reconciliation is a ministry, not a possession!

## *Be* IN THE QUESTIONS

1. How do life's struggles and high points give you opportunities to discuss your faith in God?
2. How willing are you to be yourself, "warts and all," in friendships so Christ's power can shine through you?
3. To what extent do you see people outside the faith as pre-Christians instead of non-Christians? Do you give them the opportunity to be reconciled to God?

## *Be* IN GOD'S PRESENCE

Help me to remember, Lord, that it is your saving grace, not my perfect life, that I am to share with others. Thank you for this—otherwise I'd have little to say. Help me to share how I struggle with my own faults and all of life's curves through your strength, not my own. Help me to share where I recognize your loving hand giving me blessings and purpose. Most of all help me to remember to participate in the ministry you have given every believer, including me, the ministry of sharing your love. Amen.

# *Weekend stories*

## REWARDS

I keep a bookmark in my Bible at Matthew 25:14-46. It is good to read this passage—about serving Christ by feeding the hungry and clothing the naked—often. It reminds me that I must be faithful to God even if my abilities for his kingdom are small. I love that in God's kingdom there are no "just housewives" and no "menial workers." We are all in ministry in our homes, workplaces, communities and churches. Reading Matthew 25 reminds me of the responsibility and also of the rewards of being faithful. Some days I need to think in terms of reward to get through, especially on laundry days!

Matthew 25 tells us to "get out there and do something" with what God has given you—kind of an adventure, isn't it? I was "just a housewife" for a number of years until one day a lady gave her testimony in church about how she had been suffering from depression. She had come to know the Lord through our pastors' visits to her while she was in the hospital. I felt God prompt me to talk to her afterwards to share my story of depression with her. We formed a great friendship, and God began a ministry. Several weeks later I was at the park with my children and a friend started to cry, saying how depressed she was. "Again Lord?" I thought. Since then, this type of encounter has happened numerous times. An area of my life that lay hidden in dark corners of shame came to light, not in my timing or strength, but through God's infinite wisdom, and has now become a ministry. Nothing formal, no fancy office, no mission statement—just me at home with my phone and my belief that God has taken my weakest area and made it one of strength through him.

Actually the funny thing about this ministry has been the impact on me. I have been healed more as I have reached out to other women than in all the time I spent in counseling. No surprise I guess, since Matthew 25: 21 says *Well done, good and faithful servant! You have been faithful with a few things; I will put you in charge of many things. Come and share in your master's happiness!* Some people get stuck on the in charge of many things, but personally I'm stuck on the *come and share in your master's happiness* – now *that's* a reward!

••••••••••••••••••••••••••••••••••

## SEEING THE LIGHT

After ten years, even retirement gets boring. I spent seven winters in the area where I live, but I hardly knew anyone in the community except the people who attend our community church. Then it happens. There are new Christmas lights on the market. They sparkle and don't use much electricity, so I launch a new career: Ebert's Dreams. I decide to import these fantastic new lights and sell them in Crawford Bay. In my enthusiasm for my new career, I overlook a lot of considerations which would make a business a success—like having somewhere to sell the lights, and a population to buy the lights. Not to worry. I order ten thousand dollars worth of lights and when they arrive I am thrilled!

My life now has new zest and meaning! My husband and I form a "real" business partnership—we even have a business number. We join the Chamber of Commerce. I become a board member with the International Selkirk Loop and we get involved with conferences of the Tourist Action Society of the Kootenays. We meet many people in the community; I have all kinds of people coming to my house.

There is one fatal flaw. I am not selling any lights. I would sooner give them away than have to ask people to pay for them. What kind of business operator have I turned out to be?

"What happened, God?" I ask. "I thought you approved of my plan." Just when I think I should throw in the towel, God reassures me that it isn't the lights that count, but building relationships with those who haven't yet discovered the love God has for them. God tells me I am doing well in business—his business! I have discovered that there is an "extreme adventure" for all who put their lives in his hands. My adventure with God may not assure me of a great business career selling lights, but what a wonderful opportunity to let my light shine for him in my community!

*Story by Janet Ebert*

# DISCERNING AND DISARMING

**Scriptures:**

Acts 4:18-20; 5:27-42; John 17:6-19; Philippians 3:17-21

**God's Initiative:**

*When the Spirit of truth comes, he will guide you into all truth."* John 16:13 *"And the Word became flesh and dwelt among us... full of grace and truth.* John 1:14

**Description:**

A person who is being transformed into the spirit and character of Christ, able to interact with religious, political and societal systems with increasing discernment, giving primary allegiance to God's kingdom by being "in the world, but not of it."

**Evidence:**

- Knows and orients life according to God's values.
- Increasingly portrays Christ's spirit of humility and meekness.
- Gains confidence in evaluating and relating to the surrounding culture, "obeying God rather than others."
- Pursues a grace-dispensing, peacemaking lifestyle, which addresses conflict, oppression, injustice and the needs of the poor.
- Endeavours to prioritize the concerns of God's kingdom over national concerns.

## *Be* IN GOD'S WORD

Philippians 3: 17- 21

*Join with others in following my example, brothers, and take note of those who live according to the pattern we gave you...Our citizenship is in heaven. And we eagerly await a Savior from there, the Lord Jesus Christ.* Philippians 3: 17, 20

## *Be* IN OUR STORY

She holds her baby close to her and sits next to her husband on the crowded hill. The teacher talks about unusual things. Something is different here. The teacher has such warm eyes and a caring way about him. They say he has come to free the people. His voice is gentle yet firm, not loud and harsh like the usual rally cries to fight against the Romans. She listens to the teacher's words and is perplexed. The humble will gain blessings from heaven and the meek will inherit the earth. Those who show mercy, who are pure in heart and are peacemakers shall see God and be called his children. This is like nothing she has heard before; in fact, everything he says is the opposite of what she has known. No talk of violence, nothing about the new world they will create for themselves; instead he speaks of serving and love.

Her thoughts whirl and her heart aches. She is drawn to this teacher. She holds her baby close. She wants so much more for her son than a life of slavery to the Romans, or a life filled with fear about laws and rules. She wants her child to always feel loved and secure. She ventures a prayer to the God the teacher talks about. "Help us Father," she cries out in her heart.

He squirms beside his wife. He can tell by the look on her face that she is captivated by the teacher's words, but he is restless. This is not what he expected. Where are the battle cries? I want my son to be free! I would give my life for my son if that were what it would take for him to be free. I came to find a better way of life for my family. The teacher says those that follow him can expect persecution and are to rejoice in suffering. Those who will call themselves his followers will have an impact on the world, but not through revenge and war. The teacher says murder and adultery take place in the heart, not just in the action. The man squirms as he feels exposed by the teacher's words. The teacher speaks of keeping our covenants with God and others, and going the extra mile. He says we are to love our enemies. Love my enemies!? What kind of teaching is this? This will never make life easy for my family. But no, the teacher says we are not to do well for reward here, but to please God. The teacher calls it the kingdom of God and tells us to diligently seek after it. He says God knows everything we need and will give to us. He calls God our Father. The teacher's words are full of mystery and wonder, and though it might seem foolish, what if it were true? What if there was another way to be free? Something about the teacher rings true. The man pulls his wife closer as he begins to consider the new way of life being offered.

## *Be* IN THE QUESTIONS

1. With such direct guidelines for discipleship in the Sermon on the Mount, what holds us back from living this out?
2. The people wanted a rally cry for freedom. What Jesus gave them was not only countercultural, but can be seen as "counter church." How do you think the Sermon on the Mount is counter to much of what occurs in our churches today?
3. How does Jesus' teaching help you to evaluate and respond to the political, religious and cultural systems around you?

## *Be* IN GOD'S PRESENCE

Lord, when I first read the Sermon on the Mount, my first response is to strive to make it all happen myself. Soon discouragement and frustration set in. "It is impossible!" I shout. "Yes," God replies, " without me it is!" "I want to follow your example and that of those who live the life you call us to. Help me to learn from your Word and to reorient my life according to your values. I must rely on you, Lord, to live and work through me. Then, I know my way will be straight even if it seems askew to the world." Amen.

# Day 2

## *Be* IN GOD'S WORD

Acts 5: 27-42

*The apostles left the Sanhedrin, rejoicing because they had been counted worthy of suffering disgrace for the Name. Day after day, in the temple courts and from house to house, they never stopped teaching and proclaiming the good news that Jesus is the Christ.* Acts 5: 41

## *Be* IN OUR STORY

We sat in the kitchen at the table with the roast so well cooked it was falling apart, just the way we liked it. As we began to take part in the meal with my husband's parents, Dad began to tell his war stories. His weren't typical tales of violence and pain, but stories of opportunities to share the love of God, to work hard and rejoice that he could serve his country. Though others in the community looked down upon him, Dad served in the war as a conscientious objector. "God before my country," he would say quietly, "God's laws have to come before all others." He spoke with such gentleness, yet you could hear the unwavering resolve in his tone. You could tell these weren't just words based on biblical knowledge but experience with God himself.

He told of hard work in the camps. He wasn't complaining but teaching us the lessons of work done unto the Lord. He told of treacherous jobs along the sides of the perilous cliffs of the Rocky Mountains that caused a man to pray hard and "literally" hang onto the hand of God. He spoke of life in the work camps and how God called him to use his spiritual gift of encouragement for the men. He encouraged them all right—with pranks and jokes that caused much laughter and lifted hearts. He invited those who were outcast and lonely for mountain hikes where he spoke of the beauty of God. The mountains became a reflection of the power and majesty of God. "God has it all under control" was what the sunrises and sunsets would proclaim to Dad.

"I am here in service to our God and country. In that order!" he would remind himself. "There may be shame before men, but none before my God, and that is all that matters to me." There were indeed times of shame, hardship and fear, but Dad spoke instead of God's work in the camps, the beauty that surrounded them and the faithfulness of God to him. Now these were war stories I wanted my children to hear over and over!

## *Be* IN THE QUESTIONS

1. How does your work for the Lord proclaim his faithfulness instead of simply your hardship?
2. "There may be shame before men, but none before my God, and that is all that matters to me." What parts of your life reflect this statement?
3. How do you serve God first, prioritizing kingdom values over other loyalties?

## *Be* IN GOD'S PRESENCE

Lord, I thank you for the stories of victory your disciples had, and for all their failures. It gives me hope! It gives me strength! It gives me direction! I want the same fervor the disciples had—to rejoice at mocking instead of dreading it; to have courage to stand boldly for your values in front of government, workmates, friends and even (closer to home and harder to do) family; to put others first so that it might bring you glory, not me. I need to take heed to Dad's words and to remember his example. Let me remember your gifts of grace, peace and mercy, and be willing to offer them to others as freely and as lavishly as I have received them! Amen.

# Day 3

## *Be* IN GOD'S WORD

Acts 4:18-20

*Then they called them in again and commanded them not to speak or teach at all in the name of Jesus. But Peter and John replied, "Judge for yourselves whether it is right in God's sight to obey you rather than God. For we cannot help speaking about what we have seen and heard."* Acts 4:18-20

## *Be* IN OUR STORY

A man was walking along the edge of a cliff when he fell off. He managed to grab hold of a small branch that kept him from plunging to certain death. The branch would not hold the weight of the man for long so he began to yell with all his might, "Somebody up there help me!" He scanned the top of the cliff, looking for someone to come. Then the man heard a voice from above him. "This is God. I have heard your cry. Let go of the branch. I will catch you and put you safely on the ground." The man hung there for a moment, listening to the sounds of the branch creaking under his weight, then he yelled, "Is anyone else up there?"

Though the joke is funny, the ideas of letting go and giving up evoke feelings of insecurity. Yet we hear them often as we talk about Christian faith. Only when we look to see what we gain by letting go do such words and ideas shed their sense of loss. We let go by trusting God with our lives, but as committed disciples, we let go in other ways too.

We let go of fitting into our world. If we are to be loyal followers of Jesus, we will be countercultural because in every aspect of his life, Jesus gave primary allegiance to God's kingdom. In his dealing with the Samaritan woman at the well, Jesus challenged many of his society's religious, political and social beliefs. Jesus challenged the status quo in many areas of society, fighting injustice and oppression with mercy and love. His words and his actions spoke of God's values.

I am challenged by the examples of Peter and John in today's reading to "let go" of other loyalties, putting Christ at the center. Sometimes it is hard to identify these loyalties since they are such a part of my life and are so prevalent in our culture. I have to be willing to really look hard at my life and be honest. I am challenged to go beyond the usual excuses I make to others and myself to answer *why* I have or do things. Loyalties can grow slowly over time like a mold you don't notice until it is big, someone else points it out, or you get sick from it. When I ask God how I can discover my true loyalties, he teaches me that by giving primary loyalty to God's kingdom, all other loyalties will come to light and can be taken to the cross.

## *Be* IN THE QUESTIONS

1. Look back over the last week: where were your biggest loyalties?
2. What are the "branches" you hold on to instead of trusting God?
3. In what ways does God call you to be countercultural? What is your response?

## *Be* IN GOD'S PRESENCE

Lord, let these words of Scripture become my constant prayer: *But whatever was to my profit I now consider loss for the sake of Christ. What is more, I consider everything a loss compared to the surpassing greatness of knowing Christ Jesus my Lord, for whose sake I have lost all things. I consider them rubbish, that I may gain Christ* (Philippians 3:7,8). Amen.

# Day 4

## *Be* IN GOD'S WORD

John 17:6-19

*"Sanctify them by the truth; your word is truth. As you sent me into the world, I have sent them into the world."* John 17: 17-18

## *Be* IN OUR STORY

One of the greatest revelations in my spiritual life was when I realized Jesus was who he was, *not* who I hoped he would be. Jesus was not a Santa in the sky who delivered everything I asked for. Jesus was not a protector from all harm and pain. Believing in Christ did not remove me from the world, but in fact it gave me a responsibility *to it*. I realized God offered me grace, mercy and unconditional love and expected me to love him in return.

In human relationships, we show love by spending time with the person we love, putting the other person before ourselves and demonstrating that professed love with actions. The same goes for our love relationship with Jesus: abiding in God's Word, loving others and having a fruit-bearing lifestyle. These actions identify us as Jesus' followers here in the world.

Jesus called us to be in the world just as he was—yet to not be of the world. As I struggle with how to do this, I see in God's Word that being a disciple of Christ involves responsibility and accountability for how we live in this world God created. It means I need to be shrewd and wise about the work I do—should I take the contract working with unethical people? It means I have to be discerning about my purchases—sure it's cheap, but what's the human cost? It means I have to vote carefully and express God's concerns in the political arena. It means I might have to speak up in the church or in a letter to the editor. It means I need to remember Jesus died for all people—and I need to use all my resources to show and tell people. It means I need to live in a way that reveals God's values without me saying a word.

## *Be* IN THE QUESTIONS

1. Can you identify yourself? Are you…
   a. In the world and of it?
   b. In the world and not of it?
   c. Withdrawn from the world?
2. Would someone be able to identify you as a disciple of Christ? How?
3. What choices for accountability and responsibility do you need to make as you live in the world?

## *Be* IN GOD'S PRESENCE

Lord, it's a difficult balance to live in this world, but not be of it. Sometimes I wobble one way, sometimes the other. Sometimes the culture pulls me while other times I want to stay safe in the protected "church world." Help each of us to hear your calling for us to live a new way—the way you lived. Give me a discerning heart and a shrewd mind. Help me to make wise choices which reach out in love to others while showing my love for and dependence on you. Amen.

## *Be* IN GOD'S WORD

*And the Word became flesh and dwelt among us…full of grace and truth.* John 1:14 NKJV

## *Be* IN OUR STORY

We've all seen dogs who look exactly like their owners or couples who grow to look alike over the years. I think there's something to the idea that we become like what we look at and spend time with. So, if I want to be like Jesus, the transformation starts by seeing him.

He has been with God from the beginning of time. Creator. Ruler of heaven and earth. Bread of life. The light of the world. The vine. The resurrection and the life. The way, the truth and the life. *Do you see him?* Not in the palaces, not on a throne, not even in the places of government. There he is—do you see him kneeling on the floor, washing the mud and manure from his followers' feet?

See how he has freed people from demon possession, shown his power over the elements of the earth, provided food to the hungry with just a prayer, healed people with only a word, cured diseases by a touch, renewed the body by an order, given mobility to the paralyzed through a command, given voice and hearing to the deaf and mute, sight to the blind, and life to the dead! *See all he has done for the people.*

But now, blood flows from the shredded tissue on his back, his eyes blur from the blood of the thorny crown and the sweat from the agony of the pain. He bears the shame hanging naked, amid their scoffing. He hauls himself up with shaking and weakened arms, gasping as his life slips away. He speaks no words of anger, no shouts of retribution—only a plea to God to forgive them. *See all that we, the people, have done to him.*

See he hangs dead on a cross. They take his body down and wrap it carefully for burial. A place is chosen and his tomb is sealed by a command of Pilate himself. The dreams of his followers are shattered—taking over the Roman Empire is not possible now. No kingdom for his people here on earth. No freedom here on earth. See his mother weep at the loss of her son. His best friend John cries and holds her, having been commanded to take care of her by the dying words of Jesus. Now all is the same as it was before he came.

But, no, wait—see the stone is rolled away! See Jesus raised from the dead. See God has torn the curtain in the temple—opening the way into God's presence for all who will believe in his Son. Jesus has done the impossible for he is truly the Son of God! He has offered himself in our place, made a way directly to God himself and freely offers the gift of eternal life. He lives! Do you see?

## Be IN THE QUESTIONS

1. When you look at Jesus, what do you see?
2. How often, and willing, are we to wash feet, pursue peace and do justice?
3. He lives! Do you live like it?

## Be IN GOD'S PRESENCE

God, what a powerful word from you—your Son. The Word becomes flesh! That the King would serve, suffer and die, and in return, despite our denial, offer eternal life and a personal relationship with God, there are no words to describe my awe and wonder. Help me to see your love and reflect your likeness each day. Amen.

# Weekend stories

## TO DWELL ON AND CHEW OVER

- Christianity is based on *grace* and *mercy* not works and intolerance.
- Christianity *equips* us for life, not excuses us from it.
- Christianity commands that we *live out* what we believe, not hide behind what we believe.
- Christianity offers us *guidance and strength* in our problems; it doesn't make our life problem free.
- Christianity gives us *internal peace for external turmoil,* not external peace for internal turmoil.
- Christianity orders us into *ministry living,* not me living.
- Christianity makes *heaven it's home,* not heaven on earth.

*What is the truth in each sentence? How is it countercultural? How does it change how we live?*

••••••••••••••••••••••••••••••••

## COUNTERCULTURAL – LIVING IT AND GIVING IT.

John sat in his home looking out the window. He had just hung up the phone after talking to his friend Robert. Robert had asked to come over so they could pray together. "I'm turning in my old camper, John, and I wanted you to pray with me about getting a new one." John felt envy rise within him. The old one was a beautiful blue trailer, something John couldn't even think of affording and his friend was trading it in for a better model! John wished he could take his kids camping but he knew there was no way he could afford the camping trip and all the things they would need to purchase, from tents to bedding. John stopped himself from letting the envious thoughts take over completely and agreed to pray with his friend.

A short time later that day his friend pulled in with the old trailer in tow. Again John felt the envy rise as he looked at the beautiful camper. He put aside his own feelings and prayed with Robert. Every time the envy rose up, John prayed that his friend would get a great deal.

The next day, Robert pulled into John's driveway again with the same old camper. John came out to ask what had happened. Robert replied that the new camper was at home and then pointed at the old camper and exclaimed, "God told me to give you my old camper, so here it is!" John was speechless.

●●●●●●●●●●●●●●●●●●●●●●●●●●●●●●●●

## COUNTERCULTURAL – LETTING IT GO SO YOU CAN LIVE.

Sam sat in his office looking out the window wishing he didn't have to tell his boss. But the time had come, so he prayed and walked into his boss' office to announce that he was quitting.

"Quitting!" His boss said in astonishment, "But you have worked so hard and we are about to make it big. A little more hard work and you will have it made!" Sam tried to explain that he was looking for a lifestyle change. He wanted time with his family, time to do things he loved, instead of just working 16 hour days, 6 days a week.

Sam felt the time had come to change his direction in life and focus on family, not just the "brass ring," but he found that was hard to explain to people when you were one rung away from the top. Everyone had many questions and Sam only had one answer, "My kids are growing up so fast and I want to be part of their lives—a big part. I thought this "brass ring" was the goal I wanted in life but God is redirecting me and I want to obey."

People in the business world shook their heads in dismay. "What a fool" they would say. "He just about had it all." People in the church shook their heads in dismay. "What a fool" they would say. "He could have helped so many people with the money he would have made." But Sam found God nodding his head, saying "What an obedient servant."

*Do you seek the brass ring of success or the ring of God's voice in your ears that you are a faithful servant?*

●●●●●●●●●●●●●●●●●●●●●●●●●●●●●●●●

# PURPOSEFUL AND PERSEVERING

**Scriptures:**

Philippians 3:7-16; Colossians 3:5-17; Hebrews 12:1-13

**God's Initiative:**

*being confident of this, that he who began a good work in you will carry it on to completion until the day of Christ Jesus.* Philippians 1:6

**Description:**

A person who knows that discipleship is a lifelong journey of increasing responsiveness to God, embracing the perspective that we are on a path toward maturity, that having a relationship with Jesus is our greatest treasure, and that heaven is our real home.

**Evidence:**

- Knows assurance of salvation, but presses on to greater growth in each of the qualities of a Growing Disciple.
- Regularly assesses growth in being transformed into the image of Christ, being content, but not complacent with progress.
- Learns to live all of life in partnership with God.
- Celebrates the high points and joyfully carries on despite discouragement and failure.
- Seeks assistance from God and fellow travellers.
- Is dedicated to "finishing well."

# Day 1

## *Be* IN GOD'S WORD

Philippians 3: 12 – 16

*Not that I have already obtained all this, or have already been made perfect, but I press on to take hold of that for which Christ Jesus took hold of me... But one thing I do: Forgetting what is behind and straining toward what is ahead, I press on toward the goal to win the prize for which God has called me heavenward in Christ Jesus. All of us who are mature should take such a view of things...let us live up to what we have already attained.*
Philippians 3:12 -16

## *Be* IN OUR STORY

The rain is endless but my rain barrel never gets full. I am trying to use a barrel to catch some of the spring rainwater as the weatherman is predicting a dry summer. Are the kids playing in it? It couldn't be evaporating that fast, not with all the rain! The rain pours and my frustration grows. I relay my frustration to my husband. "Check the barrel—there must be a leak," he responds. I run out in the rain and give the barrel a quick glance; nothing is obviously wrong. Finally the sun comes out one afternoon so I decide to check out the barrel carefully. Sure enough, there is a board broken at the back and each time the water reaches that level, out it pours! I check the other slats and they are in pretty good shape, so it is just this one board that is causing the entire problem. Because of one break that I hadn't noticed, weeks of precious life-giving water for my garden have spilled out on the rocks. I repair the broken board. Unless all the slats are made whole, I will never get the barrel filled and there won't be enough water to help water my garden during a drought.

## *Be* IN THE QUESTIONS

1. In our spiritual growth, one weak area can hold us back from reaching our full potential. Do you take time to check and do repairs?
2. We would never build a barrel with one or two really tall boards and a few short or broken ones, so why do we expect to "grow" and "be filled" as Christians by focusing on only one or two areas of discipleship?
3. Think over each of the qualities of a growing disciple and ask God to help you in the areas he reveals as low or broken.

## *Be* IN GOD'S PRESENCE

Lord, I want so much to be filled with your Spirit. This cannot happen if areas of my discipleship are low or broken. Holy Spirit, guide me to the areas that need your touch, and let's work together on fixing them. I want to be made whole through Jesus Christ, perfected by my faith in Jesus and open to drink in as much of God's Spirit as you are willing to pour out. Amen.

# Day 2

## Be IN GOD'S WORD

Philippians 3: 7-11

*But whatever was to my profit I now consider loss for the sake of Christ. What is more, I consider everything a loss compared to the surpassing greatness of knowing Christ Jesus my Lord, for whose sake I have lost all things. I consider them rubbish, that I may gain Christ.* Philippians 3:7,8

## Be IN OUR STORY

I am preparing for the race of a lifetime—the Boston Marathon! I have wanted to compete in this race for so long! I have trained for many marathons—but this, this is the marathon!

I am making sure I will do my best. I have hired a coach to guide me and a physiotherapist to help prevent injuries. I have found a training group for support. I am ready to train! I am eager to run! I harbor in my heart the hope of a great finish!

Then my training begins with disappointment: my coach insists I take a day off every week to rest. I argue that I will rest after the race—there's only so much time until race day. The coach is insistent, "If you do not take a day off to rest, you will never fully benefit from all of the training. It is in rest that muscles repair themselves, and you become stronger and fitter. Rest or you won't make it." Grudgingly, I acquiesce.

My training schedule is varied. I must train hard for a few weeks and then slow down for a week. Then I train even harder and then slow down again. I talk to the other athletes, since this seems foolish. The pace should be steady uphill growth, I protest. "Actually not," says one of the athletes who has run this marathon three times before. "Training is like a series of mountains, you work towards the peak, but then slow down. Then comes the next mountain and the next valley. But each mountain peak gets higher and each valley doesn't go as low, so you make progress. This is the best way to improve your fitness." I listen to the voice of experience, but I am unsure. I have a lifelong dream riding on this, and I do not want to fail.

Time passes and I train with great enthusiasm. When my schedule says to run for four hours, I run five. When it says to work out for an hour, I double it. There are times when I am exhausted, but I push my way through—I am going to be ready for this race.

But, as my training progresses, the easy runs become difficult and the long runs become almost impossible. Then one day I just can't complete the scheduled run. After long discussion (and confession on my part), the coach tells me I have overdone it and now need to take a few weeks of rest to let my body recover before training again. I am very frustrated! I feel like I am moving backward, not forward. The coach chastises me: "You are like a boat on a raging sea; stop following every fad that comes along or you won't know which way you're going! Set a healthy course and follow it. Stop trying to be ready for the race tomorrow." I feel humbled and humiliated but this time I listen as he continues. "You have many weeks left of training. It is a gradual progression, not an immediate change. Think of *training* as a marathon, not a sprint. Go at it slow and steady!"

It is one month until race day. I am training hard but taking very good care of myself this time! Everything I do focuses around the one goal—the race. Just when the goal is so close I can taste it, the coach says it is time to taper for the race. "Don't make the mistake of pushing right to the end or you will have nothing to give on race day." I think through the advice. I am not sure I believe it, but my experience of pushing myself and not listening to the coach tells me to do what I am told.

The big day finally comes. "This is what we have worked hard for!" the coach says. "Focus on the finish. Throw out of your mind anything that will hinder you—you have trained, you are prepared, you can handle anything. Now, enjoy every moment of what you have worked for!"

My spirit soars as I stand in the excited throngs of people. I feel like I have won and we haven't even started the race! But, now the goal is in sight and I am ready! The gun goes off!

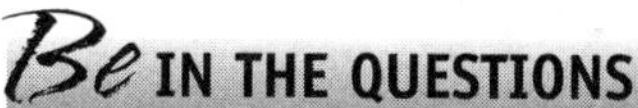

## Be IN THE QUESTIONS

1. In your walk with God do you push too hard, following every fad, or do you have a well-balanced plan for steady growth toward maturity?
2. When you think of being in the spiritual race, is your mind focused on the goal? If not, what are you focused on that may hinder you?
3. Do you see yourself as content in your walk with God, letting God lead, or are you always striving, deciding for yourself what you need to change? Or are you complacent?

## Be IN GOD'S PRESENCE

Lord, it is important to be content in our journey with you. Help me to remember that life and spiritual maturity cannot be instantly perfected. Keep me also from complacency, not caring about my growth and maturity. Like the runner, I need a good leader and others who follow you to support and encourage me along the way. Help me to have a balanced and well thought out plan to grow and mature as a disciple of Christ. Let me not grow weary from over doing it, or become complacent from not putting enough effort into the training. Lord, I want to be prepared, trained, sustained, focused on the goal: an eternity in your presence. That is a race worth training for and being in...no matter the cost! Amen.

# Day 3

## *Be* IN GOD'S WORD

Colossians 3: 5 - 17

*Let the word of Christ dwell in you richly as you teach and admonish one another with all wisdom, and as you sing psalms, hymns and spiritual songs with gratitude in your hearts to God. And whatever you do, whether in work or deed, do it all in the name of the Lord Jesus, giving thanks to God the Father through him.*
Colossians 3:16 -17

## *Be* IN OUR STORY

What happened? Only hours ago it was a regular day! I had been working on the construction site thinking about going home for supper. I had visions of a warm meal with my wife, seven months pregnant, and our two toddlers. We had plans to get our one-year-old son's photos taken but my wife had been experiencing sharp cramps all day and so we decided to head into the hospital to be safe. *Safe?* Now I sat in the emergency room, my wife and unborn child fighting for their lives. My mind couldn't take it all in. "Surely no one dies in childbirth in our day and age," I said to myself. Then I heard one of the staff say, "We can't find the baby's heartbeat; let's worry about saving the mom." Saving the mom? My wife?

What came to my mind in those moments of desperation were words from the Psalms I had always skimmed over, but which now struck me as practical: *Turn, O LORD, and deliver me...no one remembers you when he is dead. Who praises you from the grave?* (Ps. 6:4-5; cf. 88:9-12) As I sat in the hallway, prayer seemed the only thing a helpless person could do in the midst of this critical situation.

A nurse summoned me to a place where I could watch the medical team which had managed to resuscitate my baby boy. Even with the masks on I recognized the key figure in the medical team as none other than our much loved and trusted pediatrician who "happened" to be on call that evening. In the midst of my desperation, it was a sign of hope. But, what of my wife?

Some time later the emergency surgeon emerged visibly shaken from the ER to reassure me that despite a complete uterine rupture and extensive bleeding, Elaine was stable and would likely make a full recovery. Our newborn son was in critical condition in an incubator, but had stabilized enough that he was being transferred to the Children's Hospital as soon as possible. The paramedics were able to wheel the incubator and our son into Elaine's room before taking him to the Children's Hospital. He looked so small and helpless. Would this be the last time we would see him alive?

One of the paramedics, seeing the worry written all over our faces, reassured us that our son would be well taken care of. "Don't worry," he said. "I was less than half his size when I was born and look how I turned out." While he told the story of his own traumatic birth, what struck us then and in the days that followed was the image of the muscular six foot man out of whose mouth the story was coming. None of the possible scenarios in our mind had included the possibility of a recovery for our son on that scale. It was our sign from God that whatever happened, we must not limit what he could do, no matter how difficult our current circumstances seemed.

After forty days and nights in the hospital we were finally able to take our son Ryan home with us. Before we left we had our picture taken with him in front of another sign—the large rainbow painted on the entranceway of the neonatal unit we had entered the last forty days. It was yet another reminder to us that God puts signs in our way to keep us pointed and focused in the right direction—UP!

Sometimes I sit on my son's bed at night, thanking God for how strong and healthy he is and I remember all the divine intervention of that night. I am still amazed to think how God went before us—placing our pediatrician on call and having that paramedic, on that shift and responding to that call—to reassure us that God was in control and was still in the business of doing miracles. I now have a business card that says, "Anyone who does not believe in miracles is not a realist."

*Personal testimony of Dave and Elaine Esau*

## *Be* IN THE QUESTIONS

1. Can you recall a time of God's intervention in your life—through divine or practical means?
2. Are you a realist, as defined by the business card? How would you give testimony of that?
3. Have you ever called out in desperate prayer to God? What happened next?

## *Be* IN GOD'S PRESENCE

Lord, thank you for wonderful testimonies of how you are not only alive and well, but in the business of doing miracles. Thank you for miracles of divine healing and divine orchestration of events. Thank you also for the practical miracles that come through the arms of another holding us and helping us, being your arms of love and help. May I be quick to tell others of your miracles in my own life and quick to let you accomplish practical miracles through my hands, feet and words! Amen

# Day 4

## *Be* IN GOD'S WORD

Hebrews 12: 1- 13

*Let us fix our eyes on Jesus, the author and perfecter of our faith, who for the joy set before him endured the cross, scorning its shame, and sat down at the right hand of God. Consider him who endured such opposition from sinful men, so that you will not grow weary and lose heart.* Hebrews 12: 2 – 3

## *Be* IN OUR STORY

It was the last leg of Ironman Canada. He had completed the swim and the bike portions and had been on the course for 11 hours. All those hours of training were now being put to the test. Everything he had read, heard and trained for was folding into one race on this day. As he came down to the turnaround, just a kilometer from the finish line, I could see the pain across his face and the ever so slight limp in his run. I ran back to the kids, yelling, "Here comes Dad!" The kids bounded to the sidelines, put up their Go Dad! We love you! signs and started shouting. He looked up and spotted us! Suddenly the stern look of bearing the pain was replaced by a smile. The haggard face lit up as his three children yelled, jumped up and down and waved their homemade signs of encouragement.

Then I saw it—his whole face changed! He had spotted the finishers' gate. His eyes glowed and his pace picked up. He went from plodding, purposeful steps to the brisk, sprinting pace of a run. You could see him dig down within himself, pull up that training experience and knowledge to make a line drive for the finish! His goal was finally before him—not only to make it to the finish line but also to finish under 12 hours with a spring in his steps. I began to cry. You had to see the transformation! If he had run through that gate and been swept to heaven I wouldn't have been surprised. It was the clearest image of the Christian race in living color I had ever seen!

## *Be* IN THE QUESTIONS

1. Do you run your faith race with determination to "finish well"?
2. How do you plan to finish your Christian walk: with a plodding pace of grim determination or the springing step of a racer with the goal in sight?
3. Every racer will tell you that *it is not the will to win that is important; it is the will to prepare to win.* If you want to finish well, you have to prepare. How are you preparing?

## *Be* IN GOD'S PRESENCE

Lord, I want our relationship to grow deeper each day so that when I come to the finish line I will do so with a spring in my step and a smile on my face as I look eagerly forward to eternity with my King and my Savior. Help me to prepare well, to persevere and to run the race well. I pray that my life will be a powerful testimony of your faithfulness through me, having impact on those who watch me. Amen.

## *Be* IN GOD'S WORD

Psalm 78: 1 – 8

*What we have heard and known, what our fathers have told us. We will not hide them from their children; we will tell the next generation the praiseworthy deeds of the Lord, his power and the wonders he has done.* Psalm 78: 3-4

## *Be* IN OUR STORY

We sat around the table, avoiding eye contact. The only noise was the blowing of a nose and the clearing of a throat. Two funerals in three days! We were numb! The funeral today was for our parents and it had gone well. The arrangements had all turned out. Many people had come and testified of our parents' love of the Lord and the pastor had given a call for salvation, just as they had wanted. They would have been pleased. But now there was just the silence and the emptiness.

My brother and I sat on one side of the table and the neighbor's two kids on the other. The four us were such an unlikely group. Their parents and ours had died suddenly. They had been going on a weekend trip together when their vehicle was hit by a truck. Gone, just like that! It still seemed unreal. Our parents had been neighbors and friends for years. However, we kids had never been close since we had nothing in common. We had been the "church kids" and they had run with the wild groups in school. Now here we were as adults sitting at the table. Finally, we had something in common—the pain of the death of our parents.

My brother broke the silence, "Do you know what I remember most about Mom and Dad?" he asked no one in particular. "The way they always had time for us. I was thinking at the funeral today what good memories I have. I admired the strength they had as individuals. No matter what our family went through, they always pulled together; would pull all of us together! There was this deep inner strength about them."

"That is because of their relationship with God, " I replied. "As a kid I thought our parents were weird—always taking everything to God in prayer and church being such a priority. When I was a teenager, though, I began to see that they really lived out their faith; it wasn't just words, it was life. I think that is why I accepted the Lord; they made me see how real he was." I started to smile, "Remember all the Scriptures we had to memorize?" I said smiling at my younger brother. "At first I thought it was a punishment, but I have relied on those memory verses so many times in my life that I see why they did it; in fact, I am thankful for it. Look, their prayer board is still here by the kitchen table." I stopped talking, and reached out to touch the last answered prayer.

Then I realized I was making our neighbors feel uncomfortable. I hadn't meant to. I was just responding to my brother. A need to remember every look, word and nuance of my parents surged within me. Love and loss welled up and my tears came pouring out. My brother put his arm around me. "Remember they are with the Lord," he said gently. "We will see them again since we also believe in Jesus. That is their personal legacy to us! It really hurts now, but this separation is just for a time and this isn't the end of the story. One day we will be together again in heaven!"

Our neighbors looked at us in silence. I had noticed when they came in that they sat far apart from each other and now the distance between them seemed like a chasm. The daughter, who was two years older than me, started shaking and sobbing. I reached my hand across the table to touch her but she withdrew her hand as if I had burned it. She glared at me and said through gritted teeth, "You sit there with your warm and loving memories! Do you have any idea how much pain I am in? I hated my parents! The only memories I have of them are of all the yelling they did, all the times I didn't measure up! Nothing I ever did was right. I didn't know what they wanted from me. They just wanted their careers and money. They fought. We fought. It was a zoo at our place and I left at the first opportunity. I hardly spoke to them and now they are gone. Gone! We never made things right! We never said the things parents and children are supposed to say to each other. Now there are just...just leftover memories of pain." She stopped talking and just sobbed. Her brother sat like a stone.

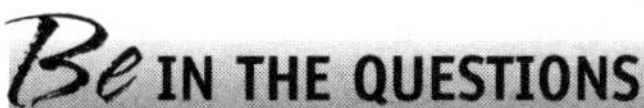

## Be IN THE QUESTIONS

1. When you leave this world, will you leave your loved ones legacies or leftovers?
2. How can we demonstrate to children and loved ones how real Jesus is in our lives?
3. How can we share a deep and devoted faith, instead of do's and don'ts?

## Be IN GOD'S PRESENCE

Lord, I pray that when the day comes, soon or in the future, suddenly or over a lengthy process, that I will leave my loved ones with the personal legacy of having known that I was a growing disciple in Christ. I want to make you real and alive in my life and to pass on that faith to them. I want to leave them with memories of a person who sought God, found inner strength in my relationship with Christ and shared my love relationship with you openly. I want to be remembered as one who was prepared to go anytime, but who lived out life with you in a real and honest way. Amen.

# Weekend stories

## CONNECTIONS OF LIFE AND FAITH

They were so involved in the church community. They had good friends at the church, they were part of several committees and they belonged to one of the most active small groups. They came to church meetings and easily gave of their resources.

Then it came! Not a bump in the road—a chasm as wide as the Grand Canyon. Their 15-year-old son was killed crossing a road at night. The doctor assured them he hadn't suffered, as death had been immediate. That was cold comfort. There was no consolation to be found. A life had been taken in an instant, and with it, dreams, hopes and expectations had been replaced by raw pain, grief, immeasurable loss and, worst of all, fear and helplessness.

They went through all the required motions of the funeral. Our congregation all prayed for them. You could see the battle was going to be fierce. Would this pull them away from God or draw them to him? It is always easy to plan a victory if it is not your war.

Months went by and they were not in church. The congregation as a whole and each of us privately continued the prayer vigil. Their close friends and family continued the unconditional support and love.

Then one Sunday they were back in church. Quiet nods and gentle smiles were exchanged by all, and loving tender hugs given by close friends. During a time of sharing at the end of the service, she stood and took the microphone. Her husband stood beside her and held her as she shared their story. Her final words ring in my ears, "We were in a battle not only of grief but also of faith. The biggest lesson we have learned we want to share with you. For healing to begin, we had to move away from the backward glance of "what if" and "why us" and direct our thoughts forward. Look at others who have been through similar things, look for the eternal in the situation because these restore hope.

"I kept looking at the poster in my son's room that read 'I love God and will live for Him' and thought, 'then I must too.' But it hasn't been easy. We are in such need and we feel such raw pain. We so desperately need to be connected to the body of Christ. Our faith is still shaky and we cry to God to help us in our unbelief. Thank you to all of you. There have been many who have stood by us, loved us, and have been practical in meeting needs of food, mowing the lawn and gardening, often without a word. We are so thankful to those of you who have quietly come to us and told us that you have lost a child and we have shared and cried together. Your stories have lingered in my ears and heart during the long tear-filled nights. Your reassurance, and really only yours, has made my heart believe there may be hope. One day we want to be able to help others with the love and comfort God and you have given us. Even in the midst of our pain we are already looking to help others. This will force us to move ahead, which is restoring meaning to our lives."

••••••••••••••••••••••••••••••••••

# The End of the Story

There is nothing like a good book on a cold or weary day, whether fictional or fact, to take you to places you have never been before, to encourage you to think thoughts you have not thought before and to challenge you to think more about the rest of the world than your own little known corner.

What struck me once when reading the Scriptures was what a wonderful story the Bible is! Often I read a small section or a single verse but to sit and enjoy it as one would a novel reveals wonderful fullness in the writing and in the characters. Have you ever read the Bible like a book? Have you ever thought about the disciples like characters in a book and so sought out clues about their personalities as you read the story of Jesus?

When you read the Bible as a story, I hope it will strike you that we are characters in the ongoing living work of God. Perhaps some disciple is not writing our experiences with Jesus to send to the world, but our activities are being recorded in heaven. We are the characters in God's love story—a story that started with creation, had a plot change at the Fall and then a reversal of plot at the coming of Jesus. Everyone then thought they knew the end of the book—Jesus would take over the Roman Empire and rule the Jewish people. But they had the plot wrong—well, actually their plot was too limited. God's plot was to redeem mankind and get back his people and his world. His kingdom will not fail. So the story continues as we await the climax of this love story: Jesus' return!

One day when I was weary and dragged down with burdens, my pastor gave me the best news of all about the Bible: *we know the end of the story!* We know what will happen after the world ends or after we die. The end of the story for those who love God is one of victory. Keep in mind this truth and dwell on it this week: you are part of God's love story. You have a vital role to play in his story, even though you may not seem to be a main character; you do not know what spin heaven is putting on the story. Remember you know the end of the story and keep your focus there! Redemption, victory, a kingdom that will not end and the everlasting presence of God and Jesus! *Now that's an ending!!!*

•••••••••••••••••••••••••••••••••••

## Be... AT THE END OF THIS DEVOTIONAL

Waiting not in slumber, slothful slouch or dogged determinism
But in quivering anticipation
Like a bride for her groom
A child on Christmas Eve for presents unknown and yet hoped for
Lovers waiting for that first touch, the first kiss
Like a runner waits at the starting line, the hard work and training about to be fulfilled
The mother going through the pains of labor
Every part of the body taut with the excitement, the anticipation
All consciousness, all thoughts, all dreams and hopes focused on the goal,
When the wait will be over and what has been longed for, hoped for and dreamed about, held on to through tears and toil, will be reality
Waiting...

••••••••••••••••••••••••••••••••••